The Top Tower Air F. UK Cookbook

650 Days Quick & Easy Recipes for Every Day incl. Breakfast, Lunch, Dinner, Snacks & More

Velva G. Clark

Table of Contents

Chapter 4 Beef, Pork, and Lamb …………………………………………… 33

Chapter 7 Desserts 65

Chapter 8 Snacks and Appetizers 75

Introduction

UK Tower's exclusive range of Air Fryers guarantees your air frying needs. Since most UK Tower Air Fryers come in handy with vortex technology, they not only cook 30% faster than other fryers but aid in creating meals that are free of fat. As such, I have an Air Fryer in my room, filling my kitchen nicely as it is the latest cooking appliance.

An air fryer is akin to an oven because it roasts and bakes; however, the difference lies in the heating elements, where one is located on the top, accompanied by a large, powerful fan. The heating element will make the food super crispy in a short time, notably with less oil usage, unlike deep-fried equivalents. Typically, Air Fryers heat up swiftly, ensuring food is cooked quickly and uniformly thanks to the unique combined concentration of heat source, the size and alignment of the fan.

Another fantastic part of Air Fryers is the cleanup. Most types of Air Fryer's racks and baskets are safe dishwashers. For those not dishwasher safe, you can use the best dish brush that impressively heightens their operationality and suitability. Since fryers are not ovens, they are oil intensive and less messy, cranking the unimpressive washing process of sides of the fryers that can be easily greased and coated. This aspect of Air Fryers is what I like very much as it eases my dishwashing process and improves the appeal of my kitchen.

Like most human beings, I love French fries. However, I do not love having a big fatty belly from consuming foods with excess cholesterol, like French fries. But with inevitable changes, we have seen the emergence of Air fryers, the kitchen appliances that have grasped my mind since they help in cooking healthy food and fries.

And this is not for fries only. The small convection ovens are ideal for food prep since they are not essential for frying. The Air Fries improve the taste of the food, and in a way, you will enjoy the yummy prepared food.

I mostly love lip-smacking and crispy food, which are lovely in adding some inches to my waistline. Fried foods are fun, but the mess comes when the food substances become oily and greasy. However, with Air Fryer, your day will be all saved, thus ensuring the appliance is a staple requirement for your kitchen.

The appliance is broadly applauded for cooking conveniently and not to mention the alluring health benefits. Therefore, within the new age of Air fryers, you may be wondering whether to invest in this superb appliance or not. As such, it is prudent to follow real experiences of my long endeavors in using the Air Fryer provided by the UK Tower.

Here, we will explain what an Air flyer, why we should have it. How to clean it? And its excellent benefits include providing low-fat content and fantastic tips and tricks to check out.

Read the following complete guide to gain valuable insights on owning an Air flyer, how to clean the flyer and the resulting benefits.

Getting to Know the Tower Air Fryer

What is an Air Fryer?

An Air Fryer is a convection oven that is amped up on top with a nonstick drawer, which is not only essentially used for frying your food. Most Air fryers mimic a deep fryer though they use no oil with more hot air and are used for frying homemade fries, chicken wings, fresh baked cookies and roasted vegetables.

Air Fryers work by holding a heating mechanism with an attached fan in the top section; therefore, when you turn the Fryer on, the hot air rushes around and down the food. The rapid air circulation creates a room where food is crisp, like deep frying without the need for oil.

Unlike a deep fryer, Air fryers bake food at high temperatures with the help of an exclusive powered fan. Air Fryers need zero preheat time to start frying food with promoted air circulation across the Fryer. With Tower Air Fryer, you can quickly cook delicious food rather than cooking it in hot fat and oil, which may impact your general health.

Air fryers are of different categories, and the most common one is the basket-type air fryer, which looks more like a funky coffee maker. Also, there are the boxy multifunction air fryers such as the Beville smart Oven, June Oven and Cuisinart Air Fryer Toaster oven.

Why should we have Air Fryers?

An Air Fryer is essential since you may have to mix up fried homemade or frozen foods regularly. Air Fryers cook conventionally by giving a crunchy and crispy coating without requiring deep frying in a unique compact form. In addition, Air Fryer will offer a unique texture and taste of roasted or fried food without immersing your food in oil.

Air Fryers are a considerate way of cooking healthy foods safe from calorie hit. You can use Air Fryer to cook foods like batter-coated chicken nuggets and crumb-coated fish or oven chips which are thought to contain many oil components. The Air Fryers help reduce amounts of acrylamide from the food you cook since frying food is linked to causing cancer. Nevertheless, they do not eliminate the formation of harmful compounds accompanied by cooking food at extreme temperatures.

With Air Fryers, you will use minimal oil cooking if it is fresh food, unlike prepared food nuggets and oven chips. Therefore, owning an Air Fryer is an environmentally friendly cooking alternative that will lots of cash in the long run.

The Benefits of Tower Air Fryer

Tower Air fryers have many benefits suitable for improving and enhancing human lives. The household countertop device utilizes high-speed fans to cook crispy food, akin to a profound frying effect. In this respect, Air Fryer offers the following health benefits, which will make you admire why you bought the appliance and never regret it.

1.It improves the preservation of nutrients in the food.

You will love to know that Air Fryer not only adds texture and crispy texture to your food but also preserves essential nutrients like polyphenols and vitamin C. these nutrients are typically compromised through other cooking methods.

Air Fryers typically use lower heat, unlike traditional ovens, which ensures that food remains in its natural state and retains its nutritional values. This is good for food with high levels of antioxidants, such as fruits and vegetables. Sing the kitchen appliances aid in protecting the home-cooked food integrity while making your food tasteful and crunchy.

2.Low calories and less fat

An Air Fryer comes in handy with pre-installed fans that smoothen air circulation and cook crunchy and crispy food by using a little oil. Because the appliances do not need additional oil, it ensures the meal is healthier so you can live an active lifestyle without undermining your cravings.

Using an Air Fryer can effortlessly savor flavored food while evading the calories that come with it. According to several studies, cooking with Air Fryer lowers the fat content by a whopping 50%, meaning your food will have fewer calories and fats.

3.Safer means of cooking

Air Fryers are safe and faster in cooking when compared to traditional methods like using ovens since it uses fewer amounts of oils. Using an Air Fryer means you won't add extra fat to your food, which is anticipated to increase the risk of health problems and heart disease.

In addition, Air Fryer takes low time to broil and bake, making you cook more food in an equivalent moment. The option is suitable for individuals who do not have time to wait further for food to cook.

4.Low energy consumption

Compared to traditional cooking methods, Air Fryers consume less energy since they do not require cooling or pre-heating. Also, it does not create unhealthy fumes and smoke, a prevalent danger with oven frying and stovetop.

It is incredible to note that Air Fryers cost around 25% in an hour compared to 40-50 cents electric or gas ovens prompting it to be a requirement in a modern household.

5.Air Fryers do not interfere with any of your weight regimes.

Cooking using Air Fryers is an excellent way to lower the calories and fat you eat. Unlike traditional methods, it uses limited amounts of oils, making you enjoy flavored food without affecting your weight loss journey.

Food cooked using Air Fryer possibly lowers calorie intake levels, thereby contributing to weight loss. It only requires a light oil coating with a few drops allowing you to satiate all your cravings as you minimize the level of saturated fat content.

The Best Air Fryers for Cooking Healthy Meals

Currently, there are the best options for kitchen Air fryers. You can have a look. Here is a look at them;

1.Havells profile Grande Air fryer

The Fryer is equipped with a digital control panel that utilizes Aero Crisp Technology, offering even air circulation for building flavored food and crispy exteriors. It shuts automatically after 60minutes and comes in handy with ten preset alternatives for precision cooking.

2.Philips Digital Air Fryer

This Fryer is packed with numerous features for convenient and healthy cooking. It has an adjustable temperature and time control. In addition, the appliance has a warm mode that makes you enjoy your meal when needed. It can create a less smell than regular fryers and is ideal for dishwashing; thus, it is easy to maintain and clean.

How to clean the Tower Air Fryer

You can find numerous types of Air Fryers on the market. Before cleaning your Air Fryer is noble to check the manual specification and directions of the fryer model you own. The easiest way to clean an Air Fryer is light cleaning after use. Also, the type of food made can impact how the mess can get stuck on the Air Fryer in cases where you cook sticky food like marinade or sauce. Therefore, when a sticky substance is left to sit on the Fryer, it will be hard to clean it off.

There are numerous items you should have to clean your Air Fryer appropriately. So, before cleaning your Air fryer, ensure you have the following;

- Dish soap
- Clean, dry clothe
- Baking soda
- Soft scrub brush
- A non-abrasive sponge or Damp microfiber clothe

As a result, cleaning your Air Fryer frequently eases your job and prevents the unnecessary buildup of food substances that can cause malfunctions, odors and, in extreme cases, fire. If you want to light clean your Air Fryer, quickly follow the following steps;

1. After you have finished using your Fryer, leave it until it cools, then unplug it.
2. Remove the basket, tray or pan and take it to the sink for washing using dish soap and warm water. Keep it set to dry overnight.
3. Wipe inside the Fryer with the heating elements with a soapy cloth, damp paper towel and sponge. Wipe the Fryer again with a clean cloth, damp and also with a dry cloth.
4. Afterward, clean the exterior parts of the Fryer using a soft cloth.
5. Lastly, after the Fryer's removable parts have dried, place them keenly on the Fryer.

How frequent should you clean your Air Fryer

After every use

Every time you use your Air Fryer, keep it consistent with washing the pan, tray and basket using warm water and dish soap and putting them in a dishwasher. Ensure also you clean the interior quickly with a damp cloth with some bits of dishwater.

After some minimal uses

Even though it may be unnecessary to clean after every use, washing the main parts of the Fryer on some occasions can help your air fryer function appropriately. Wipe down the exterior of the Fryer by using a damp cloth and check the heating coil if there is any residue or oil.

Tips and tricks for Tower Air Fryer

Before purchasing Air, Fryers must consider essential tips and tricks that seamlessly smoothen your cooking undertakings. You may love eating French fries, which are considered to contain high cholesterol, but with the recent arrival of Air Fryer, you can now be assured of healthy French fries. With Air Fryers, you can prepare food of all kinds in different ways. Therefore, consider the following tips and tricks when using an Air Fryer.

1.Do not overload

Essentially, an Air Fryer is a small oven. Cooking with it, sometimes when you are cooking chicken breasts in the regular oven, means you will be forced to stack the food on top of each other. With this scenario, you will force to overload the basket, which is unsuitable for the Fryer.

However, some fryers come with a rack where you can add food on the second layer above the basket. With this, you can cook, let's say, four pieces of salmon, unlike two of them.

2.Get used to oven recipes.

Would you need to make your old favorite food in the Air Fryer typically? That is not a task to reckon. You will need to adapt well to every recipe to utilize the Fryer. You will only lower the fryer cooking temperatures to about 25 degrees Fahrenheit.

For instance, if the oven recipe utilizes 350 Fahrenheit (176 degrees Celsius), you can set the Fryer at 325 Fahrenheit (160 degrees Celsius). Equally, you will require 20% less cooking time which can vary depending on the food being cooked.

3.Choose the right size.

If you are planning to buy an Air Fryer, the best decision is to check the size. Sizes of fryers are usually measured in Quartz, with the smallest size being around 2.75 and the most extensive measuring about 6. When choosing the size, consider your family size with respect to available models to suit your home.

The size of an Air Fryer comes in handy with the counter spacing, which is vital in accommodating food items.

4.Get shaky with the type you need

When cooking fries, veggies, chicken nuggets or tater tots, you will need to shake the basket once in the cooking process. This will allow the free circulation of hot air around the surface of the portion of food in an even manner. Even though most recipes require shaking halfway in cooking time, I encourage you to do it frequently, like after 4-6 minutes.

5.Consider owning a French fry cutter.

Air Fryers do best when the sizes of a portion of potato are uniform, unlike cutting by hand. Buying a cutter is the best way to ease your working on spuds within a short period. I have tried the Eeo stainless steel cutter for several years, which is worth a darn.

6.Think more than frying alone

Let's take a case where your Fryer is not being used to prepare; you can also use the Air Fryer to make other things. Here is a list of recipes you can give a try;

- Pita-bread pizza
- Brussels sprouts

- Molten lava cakes
- Roasted corn within the cob

UK Tower Air fryers are the unmatchable cooking appliances in the modern world. The fryers provide part of a healthy lifestyle as it reduces the amount of fat content in food. You will use a little energy as you relish crunchy and crispy fried food. That will save you a lot of money and improve your health alongside lower energy consumption in your home.

If you need to lower the level of cholesterol you consume, it is wise to check for current Air fryers from UK Tower, and all your worries will be kept at bay. Keep your Air Fryer clean to reduce the effects of corrosion, bad odor and greasy coatings.

Chapter 2 Breakfasts

Parmesan Sausage Egg Muffins

Serves 4
Cook time: 20 minutes

INGREDIENTS

- 170 g Italian-seasoned sausage, sliced
- 6 eggs
- 30 ml double cream
- Salt and ground black pepper, to taste
- 85 g Parmesan cheese, grated

DIRECTIONS

1. Preheat the air fryer to 176ºC. Grease a muffin pan.
2. Put the sliced sausage in the muffin pan.
3. Beat the eggs with the cream in a bowl and season with salt and pepper.
4. Pour half of the mixture over the sausages in the pan.
5. Sprinkle with cheese and the remaining egg mixture.
6. Bake in the preheated air fryer for 20 minutes or until set.
7. Serve immediately.

Classic British Breakfast

Serves 2
Cook time: 25 minutes

INGREDIENTS

- 235 ml potatoes, sliced and diced
- 475 ml baked beans
- 2 eggs
- 1 tablespoon olive oil
- 1 sausage
- Salt, to taste

DIRECTIONS

1. Preheat the air fryer to 200ºC and allow to warm.
2. Break the eggs onto a baking dish and sprinkle with salt.
3. Lay the beans on the dish, next to the eggs.
4. In a bowl, coat the potatoes with the olive oil. Sprinkle with salt.
5. Transfer the bowl of potato slices to the air fryer and bake for 10 minutes.

6. Swap out the bowl of potatoes for the dish containing the eggs and beans. Bake for another 10 minutes. Cover the potatoes with parchment paper.
7. Slice up the sausage and throw the slices on top of the beans and eggs. Bake for another 5 minutes.
8. Serve with the potatoes.

Onion Omelette

Serves 2
Cook time: 12 minutes

INGREDIENTS

- 3 eggs
- Salt and ground black pepper, to taste
- ½ teaspoons soy sauce
- 1 large onion, chopped
- 2 tablespoons grated Cheddar cheese
- Cooking spray

DIRECTIONS

1. Preheat the air fryer to 180ºC.
2. In a bowl, whisk together the eggs, salt, pepper, and soy sauce.
3. Spritz a small pan with cooking spray. Spread the chopped onion across the bottom of the pan, then transfer the pan to the air fryer.
4. Bake in the preheated air fryer for 6 minutes or until the onion is translucent.
5. Add the egg mixture on top of the onions to coat well. Add the cheese on top, then continue baking for another 6 minutes.
6. Allow to cool before serving.

Easy Sausage Pizza

Serves 4
Cook time: 6 minutes

INGREDIENTS

- 2 tablespoons ketchup
- 1 pitta bread
- 80 ml sausage meat
- 230 g Mozzarella cheese
- 1 teaspoon garlic powder
- 1 tablespoon olive oil

DIRECTIONS

1. Preheat the air fryer to 172ºC.

2. Spread the ketchup over the pitta bread.

3. Top with the sausage meat and cheese. Sprinkle with the garlic powder and olive oil.

4. Put the pizza in the air fryer basket and bake for 6 minutes.

5. Serve warm.

Golden Avocado Tempura

Serves 4

Cook time: 10 minutes

INGREDIENTS

- 120 ml bread crumbs
- ½ teaspoons salt
- 1 Haas avocado, pitted, peeled and sliced
- Liquid from 1 can white beans

DIRECTIONS

1. Preheat the air fryer to 176°C.

2. Mix the bread crumbs and salt in a shallow bowl until well-incorporated.

3. Dip the avocado slices in the bean liquid, then into the bread crumbs.

4. Put the avocados in the air fryer, taking care not to overlap any slices, and air fry for 10 minutes, giving the basket a good shake at the halfway point.

5. Serve immediately.

Kale and Potato Nuggets

Serves 4

Cook time: 18 minutes

INGREDIENTS

- 1 teaspoon extra virgin olive oil
- 1 clove garlic, minced
- 1 L kale, rinsed and chopped
- 475 ml potatoes, boiled and mashed
- 30 ml milk
- Salt and ground black pepper, to taste
- Cooking spray

DIRECTIONS

1. Preheat the air fryer to 200°C.

2. In a skillet over medium heat, sauté the garlic in the olive oil, until it turns golden brown. Sauté with the kale for an additional 3 minutes and remove from the heat.

3. Mix the mashed potatoes, kale and garlic in a bowl. Pour in the milk and sprinkle with salt and

pepper.

4. Shape the mixture into nuggets and spritz with cooking spray.

5. Put in the air fryer basket and air fry for 15 minutes, flip the nuggets halfway through cooking to make sure the nuggets fry evenly.

6. Serve immediately.

Potatoes Lyonnaise

Serves 4
Cook time: 31 minutes

INGREDIENTS

- 1 sweet/mild onion, sliced
- 1 teaspoon butter, melted
- 1 teaspoon brown sugar
- 2 large white potatoes (about 450 g in total), sliced ½-inch thick
- 1 tablespoon vegetable oil
- Salt and freshly ground black pepper, to taste

DIRECTIONS

1. Preheat the air fryer to 188°C.

2. Toss the sliced onions, melted butter and brown sugar together in the air fryer basket. Air fry for 8 minutes, shaking the basket occasionally to help the onions cook evenly.

3. While the onions are cooking, bring a saucepan of salted water to a boil on the stovetop. Parcook the potatoes in boiling water for 3 minutes. Drain the potatoes and pat them dry with a clean kitchen towel.

4. Add the potatoes to the onions in the air fryer basket and drizzle with vegetable oil. Toss to coat the potatoes with the oil and season with salt and freshly ground black pepper.

5. Increase the air fryer temperature to 204°C and air fry for 20 minutes, tossing the vegetables a few times during the cooking time to help the potatoes brown evenly.

6. Season with salt and freshly ground black pepper and serve warm.

All-in-One Toast

Serves 1
Cook time: 10 minutes

INGREDIENTS

- 1 strip bacon, diced
- 1 slice 1-inch thick bread
- 1 egg
- Salt and freshly ground black pepper, to taste
- 60 ml grated Monterey Jack or Chedday cheese

DIRECTIONS

1. Preheat the air fryer to 204°C.
2. Air fry the bacon for 3 minutes, shaking the basket once or twice while it cooks. Remove the bacon to a paper towel lined plate and set aside.
3. Use a sharp paring knife to score a large circle in the middle of the slice of bread, cutting halfway through, but not all the way through to the cutting board. Press down on the circle in the center of the bread slice to create an indentation.
4. Transfer the slice of bread, hole side up, to the air fryer basket. Crack the egg into the center of the bread, and season with salt and pepper.
5. Adjust the air fryer temperature to 192°C and air fry for 5 minutes. Sprinkle the grated cheese around the edges of the bread, leaving the center of the yolk uncovered, and top with the cooked bacon. Press the cheese and bacon into the bread lightly to help anchor it to the bread and prevent it from blowing around in the air fryer.
6. Air fry for one or two more minutes, just to melt the cheese and finish cooking the egg. Serve immediately.

Peppered Maple Bacon Knots

Serves 6
Cook time: 7 to 8 minutes

INGREDIENTS

- 450 g maple smoked/cured bacon rashers
- 60 ml maple syrup
- 60 ml brown sugar
- Coarsely cracked black peppercorns, to taste

DIRECTIONS

1. Preheat the air fryer to 200°C.
2. On a clean work surface, tie each bacon strip in a loose knot.
3. Stir together the maple syrup and brown sugar in a bowl. Generously brush this mixture over the bacon knots.
4. Working in batches, arrange the bacon knots in the air fryer basket. Sprinkle with the coarsely cracked black peppercorns.
5. Air fry for 5 minutes. Flip the bacon knots and continue cooking for 2 to 3 minutes more, or until the bacon is crisp.
6. Remove from the basket to a paper towel-lined plate. Repeat with the remaining bacon knots.
7. Let the bacon knots cool for a few minutes and serve warm.

Tomato and Mozzarella Bruschetta

Serves 1
Cook time: 4 minutes

INGREDIENTS

- 6 small loaf slices
- 120 ml tomatoes, finely chopped
- 85 g Mozzarella cheese, grated
- 1 tablespoon fresh basil, chopped
- 1 tablespoon olive oil

DIRECTIONS

1. Preheat the air fryer to 176ºC.
2. Put the loaf slices inside the air fryer and air fry for about 3 minutes.
3. Add the tomato, Mozzarella, basil, and olive oil on top.
4. Air fry for an additional minute before serving.

Gold Avocado

Serves 4
Cook time: 6 minutes

INGREDIENTS

- 2 large avocados, sliced
- ¼ teaspoon paprika
- Salt and ground black pepper, to taste
- 120 ml flour
- 2 eggs, beaten
- 235 ml bread crumbs

DIRECTIONS

1. Preheat the air fryer to 204ºC.
2. Sprinkle paprika, salt and pepper on the slices of avocado.
3. Lightly coat the avocados with flour. Dredge them in the eggs, before covering with bread crumbs.
4. Transfer to the air fryer and air fry for 6 minutes.
5. Serve warm.

Bacon Eggs on the Go

Serves 1
Cook time: 15 minutes

INGREDIENTS

- 2 eggs
- 110 g bacon, cooked
- Salt and ground black pepper, to taste

DIRECTIONS

1. Preheat the air fryer to 204ºC. Put liners in a regular cupcake tin.
2. Crack an egg into each of the cups and add the bacon. Season with some pepper and salt.
3. Bake in the preheated air fryer for 15 minutes, or until the eggs are set. Serve warm.

Turkey Breakfast Sausage Patties

Serves 4
Cook time: 10 minutes

INGREDIENTS

- 1 tablespoon chopped fresh thyme
- 1 tablespoon chopped fresh sage
- 1¼ teaspoons coarse or flaky salt
- 1 teaspoon chopped fennel seeds
- ¾ teaspoon smoked paprika
- ½ teaspoon onion granules
- ½ teaspoon garlic powder
- ⅛ teaspoon crushed red pepper flakes
- ⅛ teaspoon freshly ground black pepper
- 450 g lean turkey mince
- 120 ml finely minced sweet apple (peeled)

DIRECTIONS

1. Thoroughly combine the thyme, sage, salt, fennel seeds, paprika, onion granules, garlic powder, red pepper flakes, and black pepper in a medium bowl.
2. Add the turkey mince and apple and stir until well incorporated. Divide the mixture into 8 equal portions and shape into patties with your hands, each about ¼ inch thick and 3 inches in diameter.
3. Preheat the air fryer to 204ºC.
4. Place the patties in the air fryer basket in a single layer. You may need to work in batches to avoid overcrowding.
5. Air fry for 5 minutes. Flip the patties and air fry for 5 minutes, or until the patties are nicely browned and cooked through.
6. Remove from the basket to a plate and repeat with the remaining patties.
7. Serve warm.

Spinach and Bacon Roll-ups

Serves 4
Cook time: 8 to 9 minutes

INGREDIENTS

- 4 flour tortillas (6- or 7-inch size)
- 4 slices Swiss cheese
- 235 ml baby spinach leaves
- 4 slices turkey bacon
- Special Equipment:
- 4 toothpicks, soak in water for at least 30 minutes

DIRECTIONS

1. Preheat the air fryer to 200ºC.
2. On a clean work surface, top each tortilla with one slice of cheese and 60 ml spinach, then tightly roll them up.
3. Wrap each tortilla with a strip of turkey bacon and secure with a toothpick.
4. Arrange the roll-ups in the air fryer basket, leaving space between each roll-up.
5. Air fry for 4 minutes. Flip the roll-ups with tongs and rearrange them for more even cooking. Air fry for another 4 to 5 minutes until the bacon is crisp.
6. Rest for 5 minutes and remove the toothpicks before serving.

Canadian Bacon Muffin Sandwiches

Serves 4
Cook time: 8 minutes

INGREDIENTS

- 4 English muffins, split
- 8 slices back bacon
- 4 slices cheese
- Cooking spray

DIRECTIONS

1. Preheat the air fryer to 188ºC.
2. Make the sandwiches: Top each of 4 muffin halves with 2 slices of bacon, 1 slice of cheese, and finish with the remaining muffin half.
3. Put the sandwiches in the air fryer basket and spritz the tops with cooking spray.
4. Bake for 4 minutes. Flip the sandwiches and bake for another 4 minutes.
5. Divide the sandwiches among four plates and serve warm.

Vanilla Granola

Serves 4
Cook time: 40 minutes

INGREDIENTS

- 235 ml rolled oats
- 3 tablespoons maple syrup
- 1 tablespoon sunflower oil
- 1 tablespoon coconut sugar
- ¼ teaspoon vanilla
- ¼ teaspoon cinnamon
- ¼ teaspoon sea salt

DIRECTIONS

1. Preheat the air fryer to 120ºC.
2. Mix together the oats, maple syrup, sunflower oil, coconut sugar, vanilla, cinnamon, and sea salt in a medium bowl and stir to combine. Transfer the mixture to a baking pan.
3. Place the pan in the air fryer basket and bake for 40 minutes, or until the granola is mostly dry and lightly browned. Stir the granola four times during cooking.
4. Let the granola stand for 5 to 10 minutes before serving.

Easy Buttermilk Biscuits

Makes 16 biscuits
Cook time: 18 minutes

INGREDIENTS

- 600 ml plain flour
- 1 tablespoon baking powder
- 1 teaspoon coarse or flaky salt
- 1 teaspoon sugar
- ½ teaspoon baking soda
- 8 tablespoons (1 stick) unsalted butter, at room temperature
- 235 ml buttermilk, chilled

DIRECTIONS

1. Stir together the flour, baking powder, salt, sugar, and baking powder in a large bowl.
2. Add the butter and stir to mix well. Pour in the buttermilk and stir with a rubber spatula just until incorporated.
3. Place the dough onto a lightly floured surface and roll the dough out to a disk, ½ inch thick. Cut out the biscuits with a 2-inch round cutter and re-roll any scraps until you have 16 biscuits.
4. Preheat the air fryer to 164ºC.
5. Working in batches, arrange the biscuits in the air fryer basket in a single layer. Bake for about 18 minutes until the biscuits are golden brown.
6. Remove from the basket to a plate and repeat with the remaining biscuits.
7. Serve hot.

Chapter 3 Poultry

Turkey and Cranberry Quesadillas

Serves 4
Cook time: 4 to 8 minutes

INGREDIENTS

- 6 low-sodium whole-wheat tortillas
- 75 g shredded low-sodium low-fat Swiss cheese
- 105 g shredded cooked low-sodium turkey breast
- 2 tablespoons cranberry sauce
- 2 tablespoons dried cranberries
- ½ teaspoon dried basil
- Olive oil spray, for spraying the tortillas

DIRECTIONS

1. Preheat the air fryer to 200ºC.
2. Put 3 tortillas on a work surface.
3. Evenly divide the Swiss cheese, turkey, cranberry sauce, and dried cranberries among the tortillas. Sprinkle with the basil and top with the remaining tortillas.
4. Spray the outsides of the tortillas with olive oil spray.
5. One at a time, air fry the quesadillas in the air fryer for 4 to 8 minutes, or until crisp and the cheese is melted. Cut into quarters and serve.

Air Fried Chicken Potatoes with Sun-Dried Tomato

Serves 2
Cook time: 25 minutes

INGREDIENTS

- 2 teaspoons minced fresh oregano, divided
- 2 teaspoons minced fresh thyme, divided
- 2 teaspoons extra-virgin olive oil, plus extra as needed
- 450 g fingerling potatoes, unpeeled
- 2 (340 g) bone-in split chicken breasts, trimmed
- 1 garlic clove, minced
- 15 g oil-packed sun-dried tomatoes, patted dry and chopped
- 1½ tablespoons red wine vinegar
- 1 tablespoon capers, rinsed and minced
- 1 small shallot, minced
- Salt and ground black pepper, to taste

DIRECTIONS

1. Preheat the air fryer to 180°C.
2. Combine 1 teaspoon of oregano, 1 teaspoon of thyme, ¼ teaspoon of salt, ¼ teaspoon of ground black pepper, 1 teaspoons of olive oil in a large bowl. Add the potatoes and toss to coat well.
3. Combine the chicken with remaining thyme, oregano, and olive oil. Sprinkle with garlic, salt, and pepper. Toss to coat well.
4. Place the potatoes in the preheated air fryer, then arrange the chicken on top of the potatoes.
5. Air fry for 25 minutes or until the internal temperature of the chicken reaches at least 76°C and the potatoes are wilted. Flip the chicken and potatoes halfway through.
6. Meanwhile, combine the sun-dried tomatoes, vinegar, capers, and shallot in a separate large bowl. Sprinkle with salt and ground black pepper. Toss to mix well.
7. Remove the chicken and potatoes from the air fryer and allow to cool for 10 minutes. Serve with the sun-dried tomato mix.

Bell Pepper Stuffed Chicken Roll-Ups

Serves 4
Cook time: 12 minutes

INGREDIENTS

- 2 (115 g) boneless, skinless chicken breasts, slice in half horizontally
- 1 tablespoon olive oil
- Juice of ½ lime
- 2 tablespoons taco seasoning
- ½ green bell pepper, cut into strips
- ½ red bell pepper, cut into strips
- ¼ onion, sliced

DIRECTIONS

1. Preheat the air fryer to 200°C.
2. Unfold the chicken breast slices on a clean work surface. Rub with olive oil, then drizzle with lime juice and sprinkle with taco seasoning.
3. Top the chicken slices with equal amount of bell peppers and onion. Roll them up and secure with toothpicks.
4. Arrange the chicken roll-ups in the preheated air fryer. Air fry for 12 minutes or until the internal temperature of the chicken reaches at least 76°C. Flip the chicken roll-ups halfway through.
5. Remove the chicken from the air fryer. Discard the toothpicks and serve immediately.

Bacon-Wrapped Chicken Breasts Rolls

Serves 4
Cook time: 15 minutes

INGREDIENTS

- 15 g chopped fresh chives
- 2 tablespoons lemon juice
- 1 teaspoon dried sage
- 1 teaspoon fresh rosemary leaves
- 15 g fresh parsley leaves
- 4 cloves garlic, peeled
- 1 teaspoon ground fennel
- 3 teaspoons sea salt
- ½ teaspoon red pepper flakes
- 4 (115 g) boneless, skinless chicken breasts, pounded to ¼ inch thick
- 8 slices bacon
- Sprigs of fresh rosemary, for garnish
- Cooking spray

DIRECTIONS

1. Preheat the air fryer to 170ºC. Spritz the air fryer basket with cooking spray.
2. Put the chives, lemon juice, sage, rosemary, parsley, garlic, fennel, salt, and red pepper flakes in a food processor, then pulse to purée until smooth.
3. Unfold the chicken breasts on a clean work surface, then brush the top side of the chicken breasts with the sauce.
4. Roll the chicken breasts up from the shorter side, then wrap each chicken rolls with 2 bacon slices to cover. Secure with toothpicks.
5. Arrange the rolls in the preheated air fryer, then cook for 10 minutes. Flip the rolls halfway through.
6. Increase the heat to 200ºC and air fry for 5 more minutes or until the bacon is browned and crispy.
7. Transfer the rolls to a large plate. Discard the toothpicks and spread with rosemary sprigs before serving.

Barbecue Chicken and Coleslaw Tostadas

Makes 4 tostadas
Cook time: 40 minutes

INGREDIENTS

- Coleslaw:
- 60 g sour cream
- 25 g small green cabbage, finely chopped
- ½ tablespoon white vinegar
- ½ teaspoon garlic powder
- ½ teaspoon salt
- ¼ teaspoon ground black pepper

- Tostadas:
- 280 g pulled rotisserie chicken
- 120 ml barbecue sauce
- 4 corn tortillas
- 110 g shredded Mozzarella cheese
- Cooking spray

Make the Coleslaw: DIRECTIONS

1. Combine the ingredients for the coleslaw in a large bowl. Toss to mix well.
2. Refrigerate until ready to serve. Make the Tostadas: DIRECTIONS
1. Preheat the air fryer to 190°C. Spritz the air fryer basket with cooking spray.
2. Toss the chicken with barbecue sauce in a separate large bowl to combine well. Set aside.
3. Place one tortilla in the preheated air fryer and spritz with cooking spray. Work in batches to avoid overcrowding.
4. Air fry the tortilla for 5 minutes or until lightly browned, then spread a quarter of the barbecue chicken and cheese over.
5. Air fry for another 5 minutes or until the cheese melts. Repeat with remaining tortillas, chicken, and cheese.
6. Serve the tostadas with coleslaw on top.

Cheesy Pepperoni and Chicken Pizza

Serves 6
Cook time: 15 minutes

INGREDIENTS

- 280 g cooked chicken, cubed
- 240 g pizza sauce
- 20 slices pepperoni
- 20 g grated Parmesan cheese
- 225 g shredded Mozzarella cheese
- Cooking spray

DIRECTIONS

1. Preheat the air fryer to 190°C. Spritz a baking pan with cooking spray.
2. Arrange the chicken cubes in the prepared baking pan, then top the cubes with pizza sauce and pepperoni. Stir to coat the cubes and pepperoni with sauce.
3. Scatter the cheeses on top, then place the baking pan in the preheated air fryer. Air fryer for 15 minutes or until frothy and the cheeses melt.
4. Serve immediately.

Chicken and Ham Meatballs with Dijon Sauce

Serves 4
Cook time: 15 minutes

INGREDIENTS

- Meatballs:
- 230 g ham, diced
- 230 g chicken mince
- 110 g grated Swiss cheese
- 1 large egg, beaten
- 3 cloves garlic, minced
- 15 g chopped onions
- 1½ teaspoons sea salt
- 1 teaspoon ground black pepper
- Cooking spray
- Dijon Sauce:
- 3 tablespoons Dijon mustard
- 2 tablespoons lemon juice
- 60 ml chicken broth, warmed
- ¾ teaspoon sea salt
- ¼ teaspoon ground black pepper
- Chopped fresh thyme leaves, for garnish

DIRECTIONS

1. Preheat the air fryer to 200ºC. Spritz the air fryer basket with cooking spray.
2. Combine the ingredients for the meatballs in a large bowl. Stir to mix well, then shape the mixture in twelve 1½-inch meatballs.
3. Arrange the meatballs in a single layer in the air fryer basket. Air fry for 15 minutes or until lightly browned. Flip the balls halfway through. You may need to work in batches to avoid overcrowding.
4. Meanwhile, combine the ingredients, except for the thyme leaves, for the sauce in a small bowl. Stir to mix well.
5. Transfer the cooked meatballs on a large plate, then baste the sauce over. Garnish with thyme leaves and serve.

Chicken Breasts with Asparagus, Beans, and Rocket

Serves 2
Cook time: 25 minutes

INGREDIENTS

- 160 g canned cannellini beans, rinsed
- 1½ tablespoons red wine vinegar
- 1 garlic clove, minced
- 2 tablespoons extra-virgin olive oil, divided
- Salt and ground black pepper, to taste
- ½ red onion, sliced thinly
- 230 g asparagus, trimmed and cut into 1-inch lengths
- 2 (230 g) boneless, skinless chicken breasts, trimmed
- ¼ teaspoon paprika
- ½ teaspoon ground coriander
- 60 g baby rocket, rinsed and drained

DIRECTIONS

1. Preheat the air fryer to 200°C.
2. Warm the beans in microwave for 1 minutes and combine with red wine vinegar, garlic, 1 tablespoon of olive oil, ¼ teaspoon of salt, and ¼ teaspoon of ground black pepper in a bowl. Stir to mix well.
3. Combine the onion with ⅛ teaspoon of salt, ⅛ teaspoon of ground black pepper, and 2 teaspoons of olive oil in a separate bowl. Toss to coat well.
4. Place the onion in the air fryer and air fry for 2 minutes, then add the asparagus and air fry for 8 more minutes or until the asparagus is tender. Shake the basket halfway through. Transfer the onion and asparagus to the bowl with beans. Set aside.
5. Toss the chicken breasts with remaining ingredients, except for the baby rocket, in a large bowl.
6. Put the chicken breasts in the air fryer and air fry for 14 minutes or until the internal temperature of the chicken reaches at least 76°C. Flip the breasts halfway through.
7. Remove the chicken from the air fryer and serve on an aluminum foil with asparagus, beans, onion, and rocket. Sprinkle with salt and ground black pepper. Toss to serve.

Chicken Schnitzel

Serves 4
Cook time: 5 minutes

INGREDIENTS

- 60 g all-purpose flour
- 1 teaspoon marjoram
- ½ teaspoon thyme
- 1 teaspoon dried parsley flakes
- ½ teaspoon salt
- 1 egg

- 1 teaspoon lemon juice
- 1 teaspoon water
- 120 g breadcrumbs
- 4 chicken tenders, pounded thin, cut in half lengthwise
- Cooking spray

DIRECTIONS

1. Preheat the air fryer to 200ºC and spritz with cooking spray.
2. Combine the flour, marjoram, thyme, parsley, and salt in a shallow dish. Stir to mix well.
3. Whisk the egg with lemon juice and water in a large bowl. Pour the breadcrumbs in a separate shallow dish.
4. Roll the chicken halves in the flour mixture first, then in the egg mixture, and then roll over the breadcrumbs to coat well. Shake the excess off.
5. Arrange the chicken halves in the preheated air fryer and spritz with cooking spray on both sides.
6. Air fry for 5 minutes or until the chicken halves are golden brown and crispy. Flip the halves halfway through.
7. Serve immediately.

Easy Cajun Chicken Drumsticks

Serves 5
Cook time: 40 minutes

INGREDIENTS

- 1 tablespoon olive oil
- 10 chicken drumsticks
- 1½ tablespoons Cajun seasoning
- Salt and ground black pepper, to taste

DIRECTIONS

1. Preheat the air fryer to 200ºC. Grease the air fryer basket with olive oil.
2. On a clean work surface, rub the chicken drumsticks with Cajun seasoning, salt, and ground black pepper.
3. Arrange the seasoned chicken drumsticks in a single layer in the air fryer. You need to work in batches to avoid overcrowding.
4. Air fry for 18 minutes or until lightly browned. Flip the drumsticks halfway through.
5. Remove the chicken drumsticks from the air fryer. Serve immediately.

Gold Livers

Serves 4
Cook time: 20 minutes

INGREDIENTS

- 2 eggs
- 2 tablespoons water
- 90 g flour
- 240 g panko breadcrumbs
- 1 teaspoon salt
- ½ teaspoon ground black pepper
- 570 g chicken livers
- Cooking spray

DIRECTIONS

1. Preheat the air fryer to 200ºC. Spritz the air fryer basket with cooking spray.
2. Whisk the eggs with water in a large bowl. Pour the flour in a separate bowl. Pour the panko on a shallow dish and sprinkle with salt and pepper.
3. Dredge the chicken livers in the flour. Shake the excess off, then dunk the livers in the whisked eggs, and then roll the livers over the panko to coat well.
4. Arrange the livers in the preheated air fryer and spritz with cooking spray. Work in batches to avoid overcrowding.
5. Air fry for 10 minutes or until the livers are golden and crispy. Flip the livers halfway through. Repeat with remaining livers.
6. Serve immediately.

Hawaiian Chicken Bites

Serves 4
Cook time: 15 minutes

INGREDIENTS

- 120 ml pineapple juice
- 2 tablespoons apple cider vinegar
- ½ tablespoon minced ginger
- 120 g ketchup
- 2 garlic cloves, minced
- 110 g brown sugar
- 2 tablespoons sherry
- 120 ml soy sauce
- 4 chicken breasts, cubed
- Cooking spray

DIRECTIONS

1. Combine the pineapple juice, cider vinegar, ginger, ketchup, garlic, and sugar in a saucepan. Stir to mix well. Heat over low heat for 5 minutes or until thickened. Fold in the sherry and soy sauce.

2. Dunk the chicken cubes in the mixture. Press to submerge. Wrap the bowl in plastic and refrigerate to marinate for at least an hour.
3. Preheat the air fryer to 180ºC. Spritz the air fryer basket with cooking spray.
4. Remove the chicken cubes from the marinade. Shake the excess off and put in the preheated air fryer. Spritz with cooking spray.
5. Air fry for 15 minutes or until the chicken cubes are glazed and well browned. Shake the basket at least three times during the frying.
6. Serve immediately.

Italian Flavour Chicken Breasts with Roma Tomatoes

Serves 8
Cook time: 60 minutes

INGREDIENTS

- 1.4 kg chicken breasts, bone-in
- 1 teaspoon minced fresh basil
- 1 teaspoon minced fresh rosemary
- 2 tablespoons minced fresh parsley
- 1 teaspoon cayenne pepper
- ½ teaspoon salt
- ½ teaspoon freshly ground black pepper
- 4 medium Roma tomatoes, halved
- Cooking spray

DIRECTIONS

1. Preheat the air fryer to 190ºC. Spritz the air fryer basket with cooking spray.
2. Combine all the ingredients, except for the chicken breasts and tomatoes, in a large bowl. Stir to mix well.
3. Dunk the chicken breasts in the mixture and press to coat well.
4. Transfer the chicken breasts in the preheated air fryer. You may need to work in batches to avoid overcrowding.
5. Air fry for 25 minutes or until the internal temperature of the thickest part of the breasts reaches at least 76ºC. Flip the breasts halfway through the cooking time.
6. Remove the cooked chicken breasts from the basket and adjust the temperature to 180ºC.
7. Place the tomatoes in the air fryer and spritz with cooking spray. Sprinkle with a touch of salt and cook for 10 minutes or until tender. Shake the basket halfway through the cooking time.
8. Serve the tomatoes with chicken breasts on a large serving plate.

Nice Goulash

Serves 2
Cook time: 17 minutes

INGREDIENTS

- 2 red bell peppers, chopped
- 450 g chicken mince
- 2 medium tomatoes, diced
- 120 ml chicken broth
- Salt and ground black pepper, to taste
- Cooking spray

DIRECTIONS

1. Preheat the air fryer to 186ºC. Spritz a baking pan with cooking spray.
2. Set the bell pepper in the baking pan and put in the air fry to broil for 5 minutes or until the bell pepper is tender. Shake the basket halfway through.
3. Add the chicken mince and diced tomatoes in the baking pan and stir to mix well. Broil for 6 more minutes or until the chicken is lightly browned.
4. Pour the chicken broth over and sprinkle with salt and ground black pepper. Stir to mix well. Broil for an additional 6 minutes.
5. Serve immediately.

Herbed Turkey Breast with Simple Dijon Sauce

Serves 4
Cook time: 30 minutes

INGREDIENTS

- 1 teaspoon chopped fresh sage
- 1 teaspoon chopped fresh tarragon
- 1 teaspoon chopped fresh thyme leaves
- 1 teaspoon chopped fresh rosemary leaves
- 1½ teaspoons sea salt
- 1 teaspoon ground black pepper
- 1 (900 g) turkey breast
- 3 tablespoons Dijon mustard
- 3 tablespoons butter, melted
- Cooking spray

DIRECTIONS

1. Preheat the air fryer to 200ºC. Spritz the air fryer basket with cooking spray.
2. Combine the herbs, salt, and black pepper in a small bowl. Stir to mix well. Set aside.
3. Combine the Dijon mustard and butter in a separate bowl. Stir to mix well.
4. Rub the turkey with the herb mixture on a clean work surface, then brush the turkey with Dijon mixture.
5. Arrange the turkey in the preheated air fryer basket. Air fry for 30 minutes or until an instant-read thermometer inserted in the thickest part of the turkey breast reaches at least 76ºC.

6. Transfer the cooked turkey breast on a large plate and slice to serve.

Lettuce-Wrapped Turkey and Mushroom Meatballs

Serves 6
Cook time: 15 minutes

INGREDIENTS

Sauce:
- 2 tablespoons tamari
- 2 tablespoons tomato sauce
- 1 tablespoon lime juice
- ¼ teaspoon peeled and grated fresh ginger
- 1 clove garlic, smashed to a paste
- 120 ml chicken broth
- 70 g sugar
- 2 tablespoons toasted sesame oil
- Cooking spray

Meatballs:
- 900 g turkey mince
- 75 g finely chopped button mushrooms
- 2 large eggs, beaten
- 1½ teaspoons tamari
- 15 g finely chopped green onions, plus more for garnish
- 2 teaspoons peeled and grated fresh ginger
- 1 clove garlic, smashed
- 2 teaspoons toasted sesame oil
- 2 tablespoons sugar
- For Serving:
- Lettuce leaves, for serving
- Sliced red chilies, for garnish (optional)
- Toasted sesame seeds, for garnish (optional)

DIRECTIONS
1. Preheat the air fryer to 180°C. Spritz a baking pan with cooking spray.
2. Combine the ingredients for the sauce in a small bowl. Stir to mix well. Set aside.
3. Combine the ingredients for the meatballs in a large bowl. Stir to mix well, then shape the mixture in twelve 1½-inch meatballs.
4. Arrange the meatballs in a single layer on the baking pan, then baste with the sauce. You may need to work in batches to avoid overcrowding.
5. Arrange the pan in the air fryer. Air fry for 15 minutes or until the meatballs are golden brown. Flip the balls halfway through the cooking time.

6. Unfold the lettuce leaves on a large serving plate, then transfer the cooked meatballs on the leaves. Spread the red chilies and sesame seeds over the balls, then serve.

Pomegranate-Glazed Chicken with Couscous Salad

Serves 4
Cook time: 20 minutes

INGREDIENTS

- 3 tablespoons plus 2 teaspoons pomegranate molasses
- ½ teaspoon ground cinnamon
- 1 teaspoon minced fresh thyme
- Salt and ground black pepper, to taste
- 2 (340 g) bone-in split chicken breasts, trimmed
- 60 ml chicken broth
- 60 ml water
- 80 g couscous
- 1 tablespoon minced fresh parsley
- 60 g cherry tomatoes, quartered
- 1 scallion, white part minced, green part sliced thin on bias
- 1 tablespoon extra-virgin olive oil
- 30 g feta cheese, crumbled
- Cooking spray

DIRECTIONS

1. Preheat the air fryer to 180°C. Spritz the air fryer basket with cooking spray.
2. Combine 3 tablespoons of pomegranate molasses, cinnamon, thyme, and ⅛ teaspoon of salt in a small bowl. Stir to mix well. Set aside.
3. Place the chicken breasts in the preheated air fryer, skin side down, and spritz with cooking spray. Sprinkle with salt and ground black pepper.
4. Air fry the chicken for 10 minutes, then brush the chicken with half of pomegranate molasses mixture and flip. Air fry for 5 more minutes.
5. Brush the chicken with remaining pomegranate molasses mixture and flip. Air fry for another 5 minutes or until the internal temperature of the chicken breasts reaches at least 76°C.
6. Meanwhile, pour the broth and water in a pot and bring to a boil over medium-high heat. Add the couscous and sprinkle with salt. Cover and simmer for 7 minutes or until the liquid is almost absorbed.
7. Combine the remaining ingredients, except for the cheese, with cooked couscous in a large bowl. Toss to mix well. Scatter with the feta cheese.
8. When the air frying is complete, remove the chicken from the air fryer and allow to cool for 10 minutes. Serve with vegetable and couscous salad.

Spanish Chicken and Mini Sweet Pepper Baguette

Serves 2
Cook time: 20 minutes

INGREDIENTS

- 570 g assorted small chicken parts, breasts cut into halves
- ¼ teaspoon salt
- ¼ teaspoon ground black pepper
- 2 teaspoons olive oil
- 230 g mini sweet peppers
- 60 g light mayonnaise
- ¼ teaspoon smoked paprika
- ½ clove garlic, crushed
- Baguette, for serving
- Cooking spray

DIRECTIONS

1. Preheat air fryer to 190ºC. Spritz the air fryer basket with cooking spray.
2. Toss the chicken with salt, ground black pepper, and olive oil in a large bowl.
3. Arrange the sweet peppers and chicken in the preheated air fryer and air fry for 10 minutes, then transfer the peppers on a plate.
4. Flip the chicken and air fry for 10 more minutes or until well browned.
5. Meanwhile, combine the mayo, paprika, and garlic in a small bowl. Stir to mix well.
6. Assemble the baguette with chicken and sweet pepper, then spread with mayo mixture and serve.

Teriyaki Chicken Thighs with Lemony Snow Peas

Serves 4
Cook time: 34 minutes

INGREDIENTS

- 60 ml chicken broth
- ½ teaspoon grated fresh ginger
- ⅛ teaspoon red pepper flakes
- 1½ tablespoons soy sauce
- 4 (140 g) bone-in chicken thighs, trimmed
- 1 tablespoon mirin
- ½ teaspoon cornflour
- 1 tablespoon sugar
- 170 g mangetout, strings removed
- ⅛ teaspoon lemon zest

- 1 garlic clove, minced
- ¼ teaspoon salt
- Ground black pepper, to taste
- ½ teaspoon lemon juice

DIRECTIONS

1. Combine the broth, ginger, pepper flakes, and soy sauce in a large bowl. Stir to mix well.
2. Pierce 10 to 15 holes into the chicken skin. Put the chicken in the broth mixture and toss to coat well. Let sit for 10 minutes to marinate.
3. Preheat the air fryer to 206ºC.
4. Transfer the marinated chicken on a plate and pat dry with paper towels.
5. Scoop 2 tablespoons of marinade in a microwave-safe bowl and combine with mirin, cornflour and sugar. Stir to mix well. Microwave for 1 minute or until frothy and has a thick consistency. Set aside.
6. Arrange the chicken in the preheated air fryer, skin side up, and air fry for 25 minutes or until the internal temperature of the chicken reaches at least 76ºC. Gently turn the chicken over halfway through.
7. When the frying is complete, brush the chicken skin with marinade mixture. Air fryer the chicken for 5 more minutes or until glazed.
8. Remove the chicken from the air fryer and reserve ½ teaspoon of chicken fat remains in the air fryer. Allow the chicken to cool for 10 minutes.
9. Meanwhile, combine the reserved chicken fat, snow peas, lemon zest, garlic, salt, and ground black pepper in a small bowl. Toss to coat well.

10. Transfer the snow peas in the air fryer and air fry for 3 minutes or until soft. Remove the peas from the air fryer and toss with lemon juice. 1DIRECTIONS

1. Serve the chicken with lemony snow peas.

Ranch Chicken Wings

Serves 4
Cook time: 40 minutes

INGREDIENTS

- 2 tablespoons water
- 2 tablespoons hot pepper sauce
- 2 tablespoons unsalted butter, melted
- 2 tablespoons apple cider vinegar
- 1 (30 g) envelope ranch salad dressing mix
- 1 teaspoon paprika
- 4 1.8 kg chicken wings, tips removed
- Cooking oil spray

DIRECTIONS

1. In a large bowl, whisk the water, hot pepper sauce, melted butter, vinegar, salad dressing mix,

and paprika until combined.

2. Add the wings and toss to coat. At this point, you can cover the bowl and marinate the wings in the refrigerator for 4 to 24 hours for best results. However, you can just let the wings stand for 30 minutes in the refrigerator.

3. Insert the crisper plate into the basket and the basket into the unit. Preheat the unit by selecting AIR FRY, setting the temperature to 200ºC, and setting the time to 3 minutes. Select START/STOP to begin.

4. Once the unit is preheated, spray the crisper plate with cooking oil. Working in batches, put half the wings into the basket; it is okay to stack them. Refrigerate the remaining wings.

5. Select AIR FRY, set the temperature to 200ºC, and set the time to 20 minutes. Select START/STOP to begin.

6. After 5 minutes, remove the basket and shake it. Reinsert the basket to resume cooking. Remove and shake the basket every 5 minutes, three more times, until the chicken is browned and glazed and a food thermometer inserted into the wings registers 76ºC.

7. Repeat steps 4, 5, and 6 with the remaining wings.

8. When the cooking is complete, serve warm.

Thai Chicken with Cucumber and Chili Salad

Serves 6
Cook time: 25 minutes

INGREDIENTS

- 2 (570 g) small chickens, giblets discarded
- 1 tablespoon fish sauce
- 6 tablespoons chopped fresh coriander
- 2 teaspoons lime zest
- 1 teaspoon ground coriander
- 2 garlic cloves, minced
- 2 tablespoons packed light brown sugar
- 2 teaspoons vegetable oil
- Salt and ground black pepper, to taste
- 1 English cucumber, halved lengthwise and sliced thin
- 1 Thai chili, stemmed, deseeded, and minced
- 2 tablespoons chopped dry-roasted peanuts
- 1 small shallot, sliced thinly
- 1 tablespoon lime juice
- Lime wedges, for serving
- Cooking spray

DIRECTIONS

1. Arrange a chicken on a clean work surface, remove the backbone with kitchen shears, then pound the chicken breast to flat. Cut the breast in half. Repeat with the remaining chicken.

2. Loose the breast and thigh skin with your fingers, then pat the chickens dry and pierce about 10 holes into the fat deposits of the chickens. Tuck the wings under the chickens.

3. Combine 2 teaspoons of fish sauce, coriander, lime zest, coriander, garlic, 4 teaspoons of sugar, 1 teaspoon of vegetable oil, ½ teaspoon of salt, and ⅛ teaspoon of ground black pepper in a small bowl. Stir to mix well.

4. Rub the fish sauce mixture under the breast and thigh skin of the game chickens, then let sit for 10 minutes to marinate.

5. Preheat the air fryer to 200ºC. Spritz the air fryer basket with cooking spray.

6. Arrange the marinated chickens in the preheated air fryer, skin side down.

7. Air fry for 15 minutes, then gently turn the game hens over and air fry for 10 more minutes or until the skin is golden brown and the internal temperature of the chickens reads at least 76ºC.

8. Meanwhile, combine all the remaining ingredients, except for the lime wedges, in a large bowl and sprinkle with salt and black pepper. Toss to mix well.

9. Transfer the fried chickens on a large plate, then sit the salad aside and squeeze the lime wedges over before serving.

Chicken, Courgette, and Spinach Salad

Serves 4
Cook time: 20 minutes

INGREDIENTS

- 3 (140 g) boneless, skinless chicken breasts, cut into 1-inch cubes
- 5 teaspoons extra-virgin olive oil
- ½ teaspoon dried thyme
- 1 medium red onion, sliced
- 1 red bell pepper, sliced
- 1 small courgette, cut into strips
- 3 tablespoons freshly squeezed lemon juice
- 85 g fresh baby spinach leaves

DIRECTIONS

1. Insert the crisper plate into the basket and the basket into the unit. Preheat the unit by selecting AIR ROAST, setting the temperature to 190ºC, and setting the time to 3 minutes. Select START/STOP to begin.

2. In a large bowl, combine the chicken, olive oil, and thyme. Toss to coat. Transfer to a medium metal bowl that fits into the basket.

3. Once the unit is preheated, place the bowl into the basket.

4. Select AIR ROAST, set the temperature to 190ºC, and set the time to 20 minutes. Select START/STOP to begin.

5. After 8 minutes, add the red onion, red bell pepper, and courgette to the bowl. Resume cooking. After about 6 minutes more, stir the chicken and vegetables. Resume cooking.

6. When the cooking is complete, a food thermometer inserted into the chicken should register at

least 76ºC. Remove the bowl from the unit and stir in the lemon juice.

7. Put the spinach in a serving bowl and top with the chicken mixture. Toss to combine and serve immediately.

Crunchy Chicken with Roasted Carrots

Serves 4
Cook time: 22 minutes

INGREDIENTS

- 4 bone-in, skin-on chicken thighs
- 2 carrots, cut into 2-inch pieces
- 2 tablespoons extra-virgin olive oil
- 2 teaspoons poultry spice
- 1 teaspoon sea salt, divided
- 2 teaspoons chopped fresh rosemary leaves
- Cooking oil spray
- 500 g cooked white rice

DIRECTIONS

1. Brush the chicken thighs and carrots with olive oil. Sprinkle both with the poultry spice, salt, and rosemary.

2. Insert the crisper plate into the basket and the basket into the unit. Preheat the unit by selecting AIR FRY, setting the temperature to 200ºC, and setting the time to 3 minutes. Select START/STOP to begin.

3. Once the unit is preheated, spray the crisper plate with cooking oil. Place the carrots into the basket. Add the wire rack and arrange the chicken thighs on the rack.

4. Select AIR FRY, set the temperature to 200ºC, and set the time to 20 minutes. Select START/STOP to begin.

5. When the cooking is complete, check the chicken temperature. If a food thermometer inserted into the chicken registers 76ºC, remove the chicken from the air fryer, place it on a clean plate, and cover with aluminum foil to keep warm. Otherwise, resume cooking for 1 to 2 minutes longer.

6. The carrots can cook for 18 to 22 minutes and will be tender and caramelized; cooking time isn't as crucial for root vegetables.

7. Serve the chicken and carrots with the hot cooked rice.

Chapter 4 Beef, Pork, and Lamb

Ritzy Skirt Steak Fajitas

Serves 4
Cook time: 30 minutes

INGREDIENTS

- 2 tablespoons olive oil
- 60 ml lime juice
- 1 clove garlic, minced
- ½ teaspoon ground cumin
- ½ teaspoon hot sauce
- ½ teaspoon salt
- 2 tablespoons chopped fresh coriander
- 450 g skirt steak
- 1 onion, sliced
- 1 teaspoon chili powder
- 1 red pepper, sliced
- 1 green pepper, sliced
- Salt and freshly ground black pepper, to taste
- 8 flour tortillas
- Toppings:
- Shredded lettuce
- Crumbled feta or ricotta (or grated Cheddar cheese)
- Sliced black olives
- Diced tomatoes
- Sour cream
- Guacamole

DIRECTIONS

1. Combine the olive oil, lime juice, garlic, cumin, hot sauce, salt and coriander in a shallow dish. Add the skirt steak and turn it over several times to coat all sides. Pierce the steak with a needle-style meat tenderizer or paring knife. Marinate the steak in the refrigerator for at least 3 hours, or overnight. When you are ready to cook, remove the steak from the refrigerator and let it sit at room temperature for 30 minutes.
2. Preheat the air fryer to 204°C.
3. Toss the onion slices with the chili powder and a little olive oil and transfer them to the air fryer basket. Air fry for 5 minutes. Add the red and green peppers to the air fryer basket with the onions, season with salt and pepper and air fry for 8 more minutes, until the onions and peppers are soft. Transfer the vegetables to a dish and cover with aluminum foil to keep warm.
4. Put the skirt steak in the air fryer basket and pour the marinade over the top. Air fry at 204°C

for 12 minutes. Flip the steak over and air fry for an additional 5 minutes. Transfer the cooked steak to a cutting board and let the steak rest for a few minutes. If the peppers and onions need to be heated, return them to the air fryer for just 1 to 2 minutes.

5. Thinly slice the steak at an angle, cutting against the grain of the steak. Serve the steak with the onions and peppers, the warm tortillas and the fajita toppings on the side.

Sumptuous Pizza Tortilla Rolls

Serves 4
Cook time: 6 minutes

INGREDIENTS

- 1 teaspoon butter
- ½ medium onion, slivered
- ½ red or green pepper, julienned
- 110 g fresh white mushrooms, chopped
- 120 ml pizza sauce
- 8 flour tortillas
- 8 thin slices wafer-thinham
- 24 pepperoni slices
- 235 ml shredded Mozzarella cheese
- Cooking spray

DIRECTIONS

1. Preheat the air fryer to 200ºC.
2. Put butter, onions, pepper, and mushrooms in a baking pan. Bake in the preheated air fryer for 3 minutes. Stir and cook 3 to 4 minutes longer until just crisp and tender. Remove pan and set aside.
3. To assemble rolls, spread about 2 teaspoons of pizza sauce on one half of each tortilla. Top with a slice of ham and 3 slices of pepperoni. Divide sautéed vegetables among tortillas and top with cheese.
4. Roll up tortillas, secure with toothpicks if needed, and spray with oil.
5. Put 4 rolls in air fryer basket and air fry for 4 minutes. Turn and air fry 4 minutes, until heated through and lightly browned.
6. Repeat step 4 to air fry remaining pizza rolls.
7. Serve immediately.

Pork and Pinto Bean Gorditas

Serves 4
Cook time: 21 minutes

INGREDIENTS

- 450 g lean pork mince
- 2 tablespoons chili powder
- 2 tablespoons ground cumin
- 1 teaspoon dried oregano
- 2 teaspoons paprika
- 1 teaspoon garlic powder
- 120 ml water
- 1 (425 g) can pinto beans, drained and rinsed
- 120 ml salsa
- Salt and freshly ground black pepper, to taste
- 475 ml grated Cheddar cheese
- 5 (12-inch) flour tortillas
- 4 (8-inch) crispy corn taco shells
- 1 L shredded lettuce
- 1 tomato, diced
- 80 ml sliced black olives
- Sour cream, for serving
- Tomato salsa, for serving
- Cooking spray

DIRECTIONS

1. Preheat the air fryer to 204°C. Spritz the air fryer basket with cooking spray.
2. Put the pork in the air fryer basket and air fry at 204°C for 10 minutes, stirring a few times to gently break up the meat. Combine the chili powder, cumin, oregano, paprika, garlic powder and water in a small bowl. Stir the spice mixture into the browned pork. Stir in the beans and salsa and air fry for an additional minute. Transfer the pork mixture to a bowl. Season with salt and freshly ground black pepper.
3. Sprinkle 120 ml of the grated cheese in the center of the flour tortillas, leaving a 2-inch border around the edge free of cheese and filling. Divide the pork mixture among the four tortillas, placing it on top of the cheese. Put a taco shell on top of the pork and top with shredded lettuce, diced tomatoes, and black olives. Cut the remaining flour tortilla into 4 quarters. These quarters of tortilla will serve as the bottom of the gordita. Put one quarter tortilla on top of each gordita and fold the edges of the bottom flour tortilla up over the sides, enclosing the filling. While holding the seams down, brush the bottom of the gordita with olive oil and place the seam side down on the countertop while you finish the remaining three gorditas.
4. Adjust the temperature to 192°C.
5. Air fry one gordita at a time. Transfer the gordita carefully to the air fryer basket, seam side down. Brush or spray the top tortilla with oil and air fry for 5 minutes. Carefully turn the gordita over and air fry for an additional 4 to 5 minutes until both sides are browned.

Bo Luc Lac

Serves 4
Cook time: 8 minutes

INGREDIENTS

For the Meat:

- 2 teaspoons soy sauce
- 4 garlic cloves, minced
- 1 teaspoon coarse or flaky salt
- 2 teaspoons sugar
- ¼ teaspoon ground black pepper
- 1 teaspoon toasted sesame oil
- 680 g top rump steak, cut into 1-inch cubes
- Cooking spray

For the Salad:

- 1 head butterhead lettuce, leaves separated and torn into large pieces
- 60 ml fresh mint leaves
- 120 ml halved baby plum tomatoes
- ½ red onion, halved and thinly sliced
- 2 tablespoons apple cider vinegar
- 1 garlic clove, minced
- 2 teaspoons sugar
- ¼ teaspoon coarse or flaky salt
- ¼ teaspoon ground black pepper
- 2 tablespoons vegetable oil
- For Serving:
- Lime wedges, for garnish
- Coarse salt and freshly cracked black pepper, to taste

DIRECTIONS

1. Combine the ingredients for the meat, except for the steak, in a large bowl. Stir to mix well.
2. Dunk the steak cubes in the bowl and press to coat. Wrap the bowl in plastic and marinate under room temperature for at least 30 minutes.
3. Preheat the air fryer to 232°C. Spritz the air fryer basket with cooking spray.
4. Discard the marinade and transfer the steak cubes in the preheated air fryer basket. You need to air fry in batches to avoid overcrowding.
5. Air fry for 4 minutes or until the steak cubes are lightly browned but still have a little pink. Shake the basket halfway through the cooking time.
6. Meanwhile, combine the ingredients for the salad in a separate large bowl. Toss to mix well.
7. Pour the salad in a large serving bowl and top with the steak cubes. Squeeze the lime wedges over and sprinkle with salt and black pepper before serving.

Caraway Crusted Beef Steaks

Serves 4
Cook time: 10 minutes

INGREDIENTS

- 4 beef steaks
- 2 teaspoons caraway seeds
- 2 teaspoons garlic powder
- Sea salt and cayenne pepper, to taste
- 1 tablespoon melted butter
- 80 ml almond flour
- 2 eggs, beaten

DIRECTIONS

1. Preheat the air fryer to 179ºC.
2. Add the beef steaks to a large bowl and toss with the caraway seeds, garlic powder, salt and pepper until well coated.
3. Stir together the melted butter and almond flour in a bowl. Whisk the eggs in a different bowl.
4. Dredge the seasoned steaks in the eggs, then dip in the almond and butter mixture.
5. Arrange the coated steaks in the air fryer basket. Air fryer for 10 minutes, or until the internal temperature of the beef steaks reaches at least 64ºC on a meat thermometer. Flip the steaks once halfway through to ensure even cooking.
6. Transfer the steaks to plates. Let cool for 5 minutes and serve hot.

Cinnamon-Beef Kofta

Makes 12 koftas
Cook time: 13 minutes per batch

INGREDIENTS

- 680 g lean beef mince
- 1 teaspoon onion granules
- ¾ teaspoon ground cinnamon
- ¾ teaspoon ground dried turmeric
- 1 teaspoon ground cumin
- ¾ teaspoon salt
- ¼ teaspoon cayenne
- 12 (3½- to 4-inch-long) cinnamon sticks
- Cooking spray

DIRECTIONS

1. Preheat the air fryer to 192ºC. Spritz the air fryer basket with cooking spray.

2. Combine all the ingredients, except for the cinnamon sticks, in a large bowl. Toss to mix well.

3. Divide and shape the mixture into 12 balls, then wrap each ball around each cinnamon stick and leave a quarter of the length uncovered.

4. Arrange the beef-cinnamon sticks in the preheated air fryer and spritz with cooking spray. Work in batches to avoid overcrowding.

5. Air fry for 13 minutes or until the beef is browned. Flip the sticks halfway through.

6. Serve immediately.

Mushroom in Bacon-Wrapped Filets Mignons

Serves 8
Cook time: 13 minutes per batch

INGREDIENTS

- 30 g dried porcini mushrooms
- ½ teaspoon granulated white sugar
- ½ teaspoon salt
- ½ teaspoon ground white pepper
- 8 (110 g) filets mignons or beef fillet steaks
- 8 thin-cut bacon strips

DIRECTIONS

1. Preheat the air fryer to 204ºC.

2. Put the mushrooms, sugar, salt, and white pepper in a spice grinder and grind to combine.

3. On a clean work surface, rub the filets mignons with the mushroom mixture, then wrap each filet with a bacon strip. Secure with toothpicks if necessary.

4. Arrange the bacon-wrapped filets mignons in the preheated air fryer basket, seam side down. Work in batches to avoid overcrowding.

5. Air fry for 13 minutes or until medium rare. Flip the filets halfway through.

6. Serve immediately.

Sirloin Steak with Honey-Mustard Butter

Serves 4
Cook time: 14 minutes

INGREDIENTS

- 900 g beef sirloin steak
- 1 teaspoon cayenne pepper
- 1 tablespoon honey
- 1 tablespoon Dijon mustard
- ½ stick butter, softened
- Sea salt and freshly ground black pepper, to taste
- Cooking spray

DIRECTIONS

1. Preheat the air fryer to 204°C and spritz with cooking spray.
2. Sprinkle the steak with cayenne pepper, salt, and black pepper on a clean work surface.
3. Arrange the steak in the preheated air fryer and spritz with cooking spray.
4. Air fry for 14 minutes or until browned and reach your desired doneness. Flip the steak halfway through.
5. Meanwhile, combine the honey, mustard, and butter in a small bowl. Stir to mix well.
6. Transfer the air fried steak onto a plate and baste with the honey-mustard butter before serving.

Panko Crusted Calf's Liver Strips

Serves 4
Cook time: 23 to 25 minutes

INGREDIENTS

- 450 g sliced calf's liver, cut into ½-inch wide strips
- 2 eggs
- 2 tablespoons milk
- 120 ml whole wheat flour
- 475 ml panko breadcrumbs
- Salt and ground black pepper, to taste
- Cooking spray

DIRECTIONS

1. Preheat the air fryer to 200°C and spritz with cooking spray.
2. Rub the calf's liver strips with salt and ground black pepper on a clean work surface.
3. Whisk the eggs with milk in a large bowl. Pour the flour in a shallow dish. Pour the panko on a separate shallow dish.
4. Dunk the liver strips in the flour, then in the egg mixture. Shake the excess off and roll the strips over the panko to coat well.
5. Arrange half of the liver strips in a single layer in the preheated air fryer and spritz with cooking spray.
6. Air fry for 5 minutes or until browned. Flip the strips halfway through. Repeat with the remaining strips.
7. Serve immediately.

Teriyaki Rump Steak with Broccoli and Capsicum

Serves 4
Cook time: 13 minutes

INGREDIENTS

- 230 g rump steak

- 80 ml teriyaki marinade
- 1½ teaspoons sesame oil
- ½ head broccoli, cut into florets
- 2 red peppers, sliced
- Fine sea salt and ground black pepper, to taste
- Cooking spray

DIRECTIONS

1. Toss the rump steak in a large bowl with teriyaki marinade. Wrap the bowl in plastic and refrigerate to marinate for at least an hour.
2. Preheat the air fryer to 204ºC and spritz with cooking spray.
3. Discard the marinade and transfer the steak in the preheated air fryer. Spritz with cooking spray.
4. Air fry for 13 minutes or until well browned. Flip the steak halfway through.
5. Meanwhile, heat the sesame oil in a nonstick skillet over medium heat. Add the broccoli and red pepper. Sprinkle with salt and ground black pepper. Sauté for 5 minutes or until the broccoli is tender.
6. Transfer the air fried rump steak on a plate and top with the sautéed broccoli and pepper. Serve hot.

Tuscan Air Fried Veal Loin

Makes 3 veal chops
Cook time: 12 minutes

INGREDIENTS

- 1½ teaspoons crushed fennel seeds
- 1 tablespoon minced fresh rosemary leaves
- 1 tablespoon minced garlic
- 1½ teaspoons lemon zest
- 1½ teaspoons salt
- ½ teaspoon red pepper flakes
- 2 tablespoons olive oil
- 3 (280 g) bone-in veal loin, about ½ inch thick

DIRECTIONS

1. Combine all the ingredients, except for the veal loin, in a large bowl. Stir to mix well.
2. Dunk the loin in the mixture and press to submerge. Wrap the bowl in plastic and refrigerate for at least an hour to marinate.
3. Preheat the air fryer to 204ºC.
4. Arrange the veal loin in the preheated air fryer and air fry for 12 minutes for medium-rare, or until it reaches your desired doneness.
5. Serve immediately.

Reuben Beef Rolls with Thousand Island Sauce

Makes 10 rolls
Cook time: 10 minutes per batch

INGREDIENTS

- 230 g cooked salt beef, chopped
- 120 ml drained and chopped sauerkraut
- 1 (230 g) package cream cheese, softened
- 120 ml shredded Swiss cheese
- 20 slices prosciutto
- Cooking spray
- Thousand Island Sauce:
- 60 ml chopped dill pickles
- 60 ml tomato ketchup
- 180 ml mayonnaise
- Fresh thyme leaves, for garnish
- 2 tablespoons sugar
- ⅛ teaspoon fine sea salt
- Ground black pepper, to taste

DIRECTIONS

1. Preheat the air fryer to 204ºC and spritz with cooking spray.
2. Combine the beef, sauerkraut, cream cheese, and Swiss cheese in a large bowl. Stir to mix well.
3. Unroll a slice of prosciutto on a clean work surface, then top with another slice of prosciutto crosswise. Scoop up 4 tablespoons of the beef mixture in the center.
4. Fold the top slice sides over the filling as the ends of the roll, then roll up the long sides of the bottom prosciutto and make it into a roll shape. Overlap the sides by about 1 inch. Repeat with remaining filling and prosciutto.
5. Arrange the rolls in the preheated air fryer, seam side down, and spritz with cooking spray.
6. Air fry for 10 minutes or until golden and crispy. Flip the rolls halfway through. Work in batches to avoid overcrowding.
7. Meanwhile, combine the ingredients for the sauce in a small bowl. Stir to mix well.
8. Serve the rolls with the dipping sauce.

Simple Beef Mince with Courgette

Serves 4
Cook time: 12 minutes

INGREDIENTS

- 680 g beef mince

- 450 g chopped courgette
- 2 tablespoons extra-virgin olive oil
- 1 teaspoon dried oregano
- 1 teaspoon dried basil
- 1 teaspoon dried rosemary
- 2 tablespoons fresh chives, chopped

DIRECTIONS

1. Preheat the air fryer to 204ºC.
2. In a large bowl, combine all the ingredients, except for the chives, until well blended.
3. Place the beef and courgette mixture in the baking pan. Air fry for 12 minutes, or until the beef is browned and the courgette is tender.
4. Divide the beef and courgette mixture among four serving dishes. Top with fresh chives and serve hot.

Spice-Coated Steaks with Cucumber and Snap Pea Salad

Serves 4
Cook time: 15 to 20 minutes

INGREDIENTS

- 1 (680 g) boneless rump steak, trimmed and halved crosswise
- 1½ teaspoons chili powder
- 1½ teaspoons ground cumin
- ¾ teaspoon ground coriander
- ⅛ teaspoon cayenne pepper
- ⅛ teaspoon ground cinnamon
- 1¼ teaspoons plus ⅛ teaspoon salt, divided
- ½ teaspoon plus ⅛ teaspoon ground black pepper, divided
- 1 teaspoon plus 1½ tablespoons extra-virgin olive oil, divided
- 3 tablespoons mayonnaise
- 1½ tablespoons white wine vinegar
- 1 tablespoon minced fresh dill
- 1 small garlic clove, minced
- 230 g sugar snap peas, strings removed and cut in half on bias
- ½ cucumber, halved lengthwise and sliced thin
- 2 radishes, trimmed, halved and sliced thin
- 475 ml baby rocket

DIRECTIONS

1. Preheat the air fryer to 204ºC.
2. In a bowl, mix chili powder, cumin, coriander, cayenne pepper, cinnamon, 1¼ teaspoons salt and ½ teaspoon pepper until well combined.

3. Add the steaks to another bowl and pat dry with paper towels. Brush with 1 teaspoon oil and transfer to the bowl of spice mixture. Roll over to coat thoroughly.

4. Arrange the coated steaks in the air fryer basket, spaced evenly apart. Air fry for 15 to 20 minutes, or until an instant-read thermometer inserted in the thickest part of the meat registers at least 64°C. Flip halfway through to ensure even cooking.

5. Transfer the steaks to a clean work surface and wrap with aluminum foil. Let stand while preparing salad.

6. Make the salad: In a large bowl, stir together 1½ tablespoons olive oil, mayonnaise, vinegar, dill, garlic, ⅛ teaspoon salt, and ⅛ teaspoon pepper. Add snap peas, cucumber, radishes and rocket. Toss to blend well.

7. Slice the steaks and serve with the salad.

Stuffed Beef Fillet with Feta Cheese

Serves 4
Cook time: 10 minutes

INGREDIENTS

- 680 g beef fillet, pounded to ¼ inch thick
- 3 teaspoons sea salt
- 1 teaspoon ground black pepper
- 60 g creamy goat cheese
- 120 ml crumbled feta cheese
- 60 ml finely chopped onions
- 2 cloves garlic, minced
- Cooking spray

DIRECTIONS

1. Preheat the air fryer to 204°C. Spritz the air fryer basket with cooking spray.
2. Unfold the beef on a clean work surface. Rub the salt and pepper all over the beef to season.
3. Make the filling for the stuffed beef fillet: Combine the goat cheese, feta, onions, and garlic in a medium bowl. Stir until well blended.
4. Spoon the mixture in the center of the fillet. Roll the fillet up tightly like rolling a burrito and use some kitchen twine to tie the fillet.
5. Arrange the fillet in the air fryer basket and air fry for 10 minutes, flipping the fillet halfway through to ensure even cooking, or until an instant-read thermometer inserted in the center of the fillet registers 57°C for medium-rare.
6. Transfer to a platter and serve immediately.

Pork and Tricolor Vegetables Kebabs

Serves 4
Cook time: 8 minutes per batch

INGREDIENTS

- For the Pork:
- 450 g pork steak, cut in cubes
- 1 tablespoon white wine vinegar
- 3 tablespoons steak sauce or brown sauce
- 60 ml soy sauce
- 1 teaspoon powdered chili
- 1 teaspoon red chili flakes
- 2 teaspoons smoked paprika
- 1 teaspoon garlic salt
- For the Vegetable:
- 1 courgette, cut in cubes
- 1 butternut squash, deseeded and cut in cubes
- 1 red pepper, cut in cubes
- 1 green pepper, cut in cubes
- Salt and ground black pepper, to taste
- Cooking spray
- Special Equipment:
- 4 bamboo skewers, soaked in water for at least 30 minutes

DIRECTIONS

1. Combine the ingredients for the pork in a large bowl. Press the pork to dunk in the marinade. Wrap the bowl in plastic and refrigerate for at least an hour.
2. Preheat the air fryer to 188°C and spritz with cooking spray.
3. Remove the pork from the marinade and run the skewers through the pork and vegetables alternatively. Sprinkle with salt and pepper to taste.
4. Arrange the skewers in the preheated air fryer and spritz with cooking spray. Air fry for 8 minutes or until the pork is browned and the vegetables are lightly charred and tender. Flip the skewers halfway through. You may need to work in batches to avoid overcrowding.
5. Serve immediately.

Pork Shoulder with Garlicky Coriander-Parsley Sauce

Serves 4
Cook time: 30 minutes

INGREDIENTS

- 1 teaspoon flaxseed meal
- 1 egg white, well whisked
- 1 tablespoon soy sauce
- 1 teaspoon lemon juice, preferably freshly squeezed
- 1 tablespoon olive oil
- 450 g pork shoulder, cut into pieces 2-inches long

- Salt and ground black pepper, to taste
- Garlicky Coriander-Parsley Sauce:
- 3 garlic cloves, minced
- 80 ml fresh coriander leaves
- 80 ml fresh parsley leaves
- 1 teaspoon lemon juice
- ½ tablespoon salt
- 80 ml extra-virgin olive oil

DIRECTIONS

1. Combine the flaxseed meal, egg white, soy sauce, lemon juice, salt, black pepper, and olive oil in a large bowl. Dunk the pork strips in and press to submerge.
2. Wrap the bowl in plastic and refrigerate to marinate for at least an hour.
3. Preheat the air fryer to 192ºC.
4. Arrange the marinated pork strips in the preheated air fryer and air fry for 30 minutes or until cooked through and well browned. Flip the strips halfway through.
5. Meanwhile, combine the ingredients for the sauce in a small bowl. Stir to mix well. Arrange the bowl in the refrigerator to chill until ready to serve.
6. Serve the air fried pork strips with the chilled sauce.

Pork Schnitzels with Sour Cream and Dill Sauce

Serves 4 to 6
Cook time: 24 minutes

INGREDIENTS

- 120 ml flour
- 1½ teaspoons salt
- Freshly ground black pepper, to taste
- 2 eggs
- 120 ml milk
- 355 ml toasted breadcrumbs
- 1 teaspoon paprika
- 6 boneless pork chops (about 680 g), fat trimmed, pound to ½-inch thick
- 2 tablespoons olive oil
- 3 tablespoons melted butter
- Lemon wedges, for serving
- Sour Cream and Dill Sauce:
- 235 ml chicken stock
- 1½ tablespoons cornflour
- 80 ml sour cream
- 1½ tablespoons chopped fresh dill
- Salt and ground black pepper, to taste

DIRECTIONS

1. Preheat the air fryer to 204ºC.
2. Combine the flour with salt and black pepper in a large bowl. Stir to mix well. Whisk the egg with milk in a second bowl. Stir the breadcrumbs and paprika in a third bowl.
3. Dredge the pork chops in the flour bowl, then in the egg milk, and then into the breadcrumbs bowl. Press to coat well. Shake the excess off.
4. Arrange one pork chop in the preheated air fryer each time, then brush with olive oil and butter on all sides.
5. Air fry each pork chop for 4 minutes or until golden brown and crispy. Flip the chop halfway through the cooking time.
6. Transfer the cooked pork chop (schnitzel) to a baking pan in the oven and keep warm over low heat while air frying the remaining pork chops.
7. Meanwhile, combine the chicken stock and cornflour in a small saucepan and bring to a boil over medium-high heat. Simmer for 2 more minutes.
8. Turn off the heat, then mix in the sour cream, fresh dill, salt, and black pepper.
9. Remove the schnitzels from the air fryer to a plate and baste with sour cream and dill sauce. Squeeze the lemon wedges over and slice to serve.

Chapter 5 Fish and Seafood

Tuna Patty Sliders

Serves 4
Cook time: 10 to 15 minutes

INGREDIENTS

- 3 x 140 g cans tuna, packed in water
- 40 g whole-wheat panko bread crumbs
- 50 g shredded Parmesan cheese
- 1 tablespoon Sriracha
- ¾ teaspoon black pepper
- 10 whole-wheat buns
- Cooking spray

DIRECTIONS

1. Preheat the air fryer to 176ºC.
2. Spray the air fryer basket lightly with cooking spray.
3. In a medium bowl combine the tuna, bread crumbs, Parmesan cheese, Sriracha, and black pepper and stir to combine.
4. Form the mixture into 10 patties.
5. Place the patties in the air fryer basket in a single layer. Spray the patties lightly with cooking spray. You may need to cook them in batches.
6. Air fry for 6 to 8 minutes. Turn the patties over and lightly spray with cooking spray. Air fry until golden brown and crisp, another 4 to 7 more minutes. Serve warm.

Country Prawns

Serves 4
Cook time: 15 to 20 minutes

INGREDIENTS

- 455 g large prawns, peeled and deveined, with tails on
- 455 g smoked sausage, cut into thick slices
- 2 corn cobs, quartered
- 1 courgette, cut into bite-sized pieces
- 1 red bell pepper, cut into chunks
- 1 tablespoon Old Bay seasoning
- 2 tablespoons olive oil
- Cooking spray

DIRECTIONS

1. Preheat the air fryer to 204ºC. Spray the air fryer basket lightly with cooking spray.
2. In a large bowl, mix the prawns, sausage, corn, courgette, bell pepper, and Old Bay seasoning, and toss to coat with the spices. Add the olive oil and toss again until evenly coated.
3. Spread the mixture in the air fryer basket in a single layer. You will need to cook in batches.
4. Air fry for 15 to 20 minutes, or until cooked through, shaking the basket every 5 minutes for even cooking.
5. Serve immediately.

Tex-Mex Salmon Bowl

Serves 4
Cook time: 9 to 14 minutes

INGREDIENTS

- 340 g salmon fillets, cut into 1½-inch cubes
- 1 red onion, chopped
- 1 jalapeño pepper, minced
- 1 red bell pepper, chopped
- 60 ml salsa
- 2 teaspoons peanut or safflower oil
- 2 tablespoons tomato juice
- 1 teaspoon chilli powder

DIRECTIONS

1. Preheat the air fryer to 188ºC.
2. Mix together the salmon cubes, red onion, jalapeño, red bell pepper, salsa, peanut oil, tomato juice, chilli powder in a medium metal bowl and stir until well incorporated.
3. Transfer the bowl to the air fryer basket and bake for 9 to 14 minutes, stirring once, or until the salmon is cooked through and the veggies are fork-tender.
4. Serve warm.

Cajun and Lemon Pepper Cod

Makes 2 cod fillets
Cook time: 12 minutes

INGREDIENTS

- 1 tablespoon Cajun seasoning
- 1 teaspoon salt
- ½ teaspoon lemon pepper
- ½ teaspoon freshly ground black pepper
- 2 x 230 g cod fillets, cut to fit into the air fryer basket

- Cooking spray
- 2 tablespoons unsalted butter, melted
- 1 lemon, cut into 4 wedges

DIRECTIONS

1. Preheat the air fryer to 182ºC. Spritz the air fryer basket with cooking spray.
2. Thoroughly combine the Cajun seasoning, salt, lemon pepper, and black pepper in a small bowl. Rub this mixture all over the cod fillets until completely coated.
3. Put the fillets in the air fryer basket and brush the melted butter over both sides of each fillet.
4. Bake in the preheated air fryer for 12 minutes, flipping the fillets halfway through, or until the fish flakes easily with a fork.
5. Remove the fillets from the basket and serve with fresh lemon wedges.

Salmon Burgers

Serves 5
Cook time: 12 minutes

INGREDIENTS

- Lemon-Caper Rémoulade:
- 115 g mayonnaise
- 2 tablespoons minced drained capers
- 2 tablespoons chopped fresh parsley
- 2 teaspoons fresh lemon juice
- Salmon Patties:
- 450 g wild salmon fillet, skinned and pin bones removed
- 6 tablespoons panko bread crumbs
- ½ minced small red onion plus 1/2 slivered for serving
- 1 garlic clove, minced
- 1 large egg, lightly beaten
- 1 tablespoon Dijon mustard
- 1 teaspoon fresh lemon juice
- 1 tablespoon chopped fresh parsley
- ½ teaspoon kosher or coarse sea salt
- For Serving:
- 5 whole wheat potato buns or gluten-free buns
- 10 lettuce leaves

DIRECTIONS

1. For the lemon-caper rémoulade: In a small bowl, combine the mayonnaise, capers, parsley, and lemon juice and mix well.
2. For the salmon patties: Cut off a 110 g piece of the salmon and transfer to a food processor. Pulse until it becomes pasty. With a sharp knife, chop the remaining salmon into small cubes.

3. In a medium bowl, combine the chopped and processed salmon with the panko, minced red onion, garlic, egg, mustard, lemon juice, parsley, and salt. Toss gently to combine. Form the mixture into 5 patties about ¾ inch thick. Refrigerate for at least 30 minutes.

4. Preheat the air fryer to 204ºC.

5. Working in batches, place the patties in the air fryer basket. Air fry for about 12 minutes, gently flipping halfway, until golden and cooked through.

6. To serve, transfer each patty to a bun. Top each with 2 lettuce leaves, 2 tablespoons of the rémoulade, and the slivered red onions.

Sole and Cauliflower Fritters

Serves 2
Cook time: 24 minutes

INGREDIENTS

- 230 g sole fillets
- 230 g mashed cauliflower
- 75 g red onion, chopped
- 1 bell pepper, finely chopped
- 1 egg, beaten
- 2 garlic cloves, minced
- 2 tablespoons fresh parsley, chopped
- 1 tablespoon olive oil
- 1 tablespoon coconut aminos or tamari
- ½ teaspoon scotch bonnet pepper, minced
- ½ teaspoon paprika
- Salt and white pepper, to taste
- Cooking spray

DIRECTIONS

Preheat the air fryer to 202ºC. Spray the air fryer basket with cooking spray.

2. Place the sole fillets in the basket and air fry for 10 minutes, flipping them halfway through.

3. When the fillets are done, transfer them to a large bowl. Mash the fillets into flakes. Add the remaining ingredients and stir to combine.

4. Make the fritters: Scoop out 2 tablespoons of the fish mixture and shape into a patty about ½ inch thick with your hands. Repeat with the remaining fish mixture.

5. Arrange the patties in the air fryer basket and bake for 14 minutes, flipping the patties halfway through, or until they are golden brown and cooked through.

6. Cool for 5 minutes and serve on a plate.

Cajun Catfish Cakes with Cheese

Serves 4
Cook time: 35 minutes

INGREDIENTS

- 2 catfish fillets
- 85 g butter
- 150 g shredded Parmesan cheese
- 150 g shredded Swiss cheese
- 120 ml buttermilk
- 1 teaspoon baking powder
- 1 teaspoon baking soda
- 1 teaspoon Cajun seasoning

DIRECTIONS

1. Bring a pot of salted water to a boil. Add the catfish fillets to the boiling water and let them boil for 5 minutes until they become opaque.
2. Remove the fillets from the pot to a mixing bowl and flake them into small pieces with a fork.
3. Add the remaining ingredients to the bowl of fish and stir until well incorporated.
4. Divide the fish mixture into 12 equal portions and shape each portion into a patty.
5. Preheat the air fryer to 192°C.
6. Arrange the patties in the air fryer basket and air fry in batches for 15 minutes until golden brown and cooked through. Flip the patties halfway through the cooking time.
7. Let the patties sit for 5 minutes and serve.

Baked Tilapia with Garlic Aioli

Serves 4
Cook time: 15 minutes

INGREDIENTS
Tilapia:

- 4 tilapia fillets
- 1 tablespoon extra-virgin olive oil
- 1 teaspoon garlic powder
- 1 teaspoon paprika
- 1 teaspoon dried basil
- A pinch of lemon-pepper seasoning

Garlic Aioli:

- 2 garlic cloves, minced
- 1 tablespoon mayonnaise
- Juice of ½ lemon
- 1 teaspoon extra-virgin olive oil
- Salt and pepper, to taste

DIRECTIONS

1. Preheat the air fryer to 204°C.
2. On a clean work surface, brush both sides of each fillet with the olive oil. Sprinkle with the garlic powder, paprika, basil, and lemon-pepper seasoning.
3. Place the fillets in the air fryer basket and bake for 15 minutes, flipping the fillets halfway through, or until the fish flakes easily and is no longer translucent in the center.
4. Meanwhile, make the garlic aioli: Whisk together the garlic, mayo, lemon juice, olive oil, salt, and pepper in a small bowl until smooth.
5. Remove the fish from the basket and serve with the garlic aioli on the side.

Parmesan-Crusted Halibut Fillets

Serves 4
Cook time: 10 minutes

INGREDIENTS

- 2 medium-sized halibut fillets
- Dash of tabasco sauce
- 1 teaspoon curry powder
- ½ teaspoon ground coriander
- ½ teaspoon hot paprika
- Kosher or coarse sea salt, and freshly cracked mixed peppercorns, to taste
- 2 eggs
- 1½ tablespoons olive oil
- 75 g grated Parmesan cheese

DIRECTIONS

1. Preheat the air fryer to 185°C.
2. On a clean work surface, drizzle the halibut fillets with the tabasco sauce. Sprinkle with the curry powder, coriander, hot paprika, salt, and cracked mixed peppercorns. Set aside.
3. In a shallow bowl, beat the eggs until frothy. In another shallow bowl, combine the olive oil and Parmesan cheese.
4. One at a time, dredge the halibut fillets in the beaten eggs, shaking off any excess, then roll them over the Parmesan cheese until evenly coated.
5. Arrange the halibut fillets in the air fryer basket in a single layer and air fry for 10 minutes, or until the fish is golden brown and crisp.
6. Cool for 5 minutes before serving.

Parmesan-Crusted Hake with Garlic Sauce

Serves 3
Cook time: 10 minutes

INGREDIENTS
Fish:
- 6 tablespoons mayonnaise
- 1 tablespoon fresh lime juice
- 1 teaspoon Dijon mustard
- 150 g grated Parmesan cheese
- Salt, to taste
- ¼ teaspoon ground black pepper, or more to taste
- 3 hake fillets, patted dry
- Nonstick cooking spray

Garlic Sauce:
- 60 ml plain Greek yogurt
- 2 tablespoons olive oil
- 2 cloves garlic, minced
- ½ teaspoon minced tarragon leaves

DIRECTIONS
1. Preheat the air fryer to 202ºC.
2. Mix the mayo, lime juice, and mustard in a shallow bowl and whisk to combine. In another shallow bowl, stir together the grated Parmesan cheese, salt, and pepper.
3. Dredge each fillet in the mayo mixture, then roll them in the cheese mixture until they are evenly coated on both sides.
4. Spray the air fryer basket with nonstick cooking spray. Arrange the fillets in the basket and air fry for 10 minutes, or until the fish flakes easily with a fork. Flip the fillets halfway through the cooking time.
5. Meanwhile, in a small bowl, whisk all the ingredients for the sauce until well incorporated.
6. Serve the fish warm alongside the sauce.

Lemony Prawns

Serves 4
Cook time: 7 to 8 minutes

INGREDIENTS
- 455 g prawns, peeled and deveined
- 4 tablespoons olive oil
- 1½ tablespoons lemon juice
- 1½ tablespoons fresh parsley, roughly chopped
- 2 cloves garlic, finely minced
- 1 teaspoon crushed red pepper flakes, or more to taste
- Garlic pepper, to taste
- Sea salt flakes, to taste

DIRECTIONS

1. Preheat the air fryer to 196°C.
2. Toss all the ingredients in a large bowl until the prawns are coated on all sides.
3. Arrange the prawns in the air fryer basket and air fry for 7 to 8 minutes, or until the prawns are pink and cooked through.
4. Serve warm.

Prawn and Cherry Tomato Kebabs

Serves 4
Cook time: 5 minutes

INGREDIENTS

- 680 g jumbo prawns, cleaned, peeled and deveined
- 455 g cherry tomatoes
- 2 tablespoons butter, melted
- 1 tablespoons Sriracha sauce
- Sea salt and ground black pepper, to taste
- 1 teaspoon dried parsley flakes
- ½ teaspoon dried basil
- ½ teaspoon dried oregano
- ½ teaspoon mustard seeds
- ½ teaspoon marjoram
- Special Equipment:
- 4 to 6 wooden skewers, soaked in water for 30 minutes

DIRECTIONS

1. Preheat the air fryer to 204°C.
2. Put all the ingredients in a large bowl and toss to coat well.
3. Make the kebabs: Thread, alternating jumbo prawns and cherry tomatoes, onto the wooden skewers that fit into the air fryer.
4. Arrange the kebabs in the air fryer basket. You may need to cook in batches depending on the size of your air fryer basket.
5. Air fry for 5 minutes, or until the prawns are pink and the cherry tomatoes are softened. Repeat with the remaining kebabs. Let the prawns and cherry tomato kebabs cool for 5 minutes and serve hot.

Panko Crab Sticks with Mayo Sauce

Serves 4
Cook time: 12 minutes

INGREDIENTS

Crab Sticks:

- 2 eggs
- 120 g plain flour
- 50 g panko bread crumbs
- 1 tablespoon Old Bay seasoning
- 455 g crab sticks
- Cooking spray

Mayo Sauce:

- 115 g mayonnaise
- 1 lime, juiced
- 2 garlic cloves, minced

DIRECTIONS

1. Preheat air fryer to 200°C.
2. In a bowl, beat the eggs. In a shallow bowl, place the flour. In another shallow bowl, thoroughly combine the panko bread crumbs and old bay seasoning.
3. Dredge the crab sticks in the flour, shaking off any excess, then in the beaten eggs, finally press them in the bread crumb mixture to coat well.
4. Arrange the crab sticks in the air fryer basket and spray with cooking spray.
5. Air fry for 12 minutes until golden brown. Flip the crab sticks halfway through the cooking time.
6. Meanwhile, make the sauce by whisking together the mayo, lime juice, and garlic in a small bowl.
7. Serve the crab sticks with the mayo sauce on the side.

Easy Scallops

Serves 2
Cook time: 4 minutes

INGREDIENTS

- 12 medium sea scallops, rinsed and patted dry
- 1 teaspoon fine sea salt
- ¾ teaspoon ground black pepper, plus more for garnish
- Fresh thyme leaves, for garnish (optional)
- Avocado oil spray

DIRECTIONS

1. Preheat the air fryer to 200°C. Coat the air fryer basket with avocado oil spray.
2. Place the scallops in a medium bowl and spritz with avocado oil spray. Sprinkle the salt and pepper to season.

3. Transfer the seasoned scallops to the air fryer basket, spacing them apart. You may need to work in batches to avoid overcrowding.
4. Air fry for 4 minutes, flipping the scallops halfway through, or until the scallops are firm and reach an internal temperature of just 64ºC on a meat thermometer.
5. Remove from the basket and repeat with the remaining scallops.
6. Sprinkle the pepper and thyme leaves on top for garnish, if desired. Serve immediately.

Cod Tacos with Mango Salsa

Serves 4
Cook time: 17 minutes

INGREDIENTS
- 1 mango, peeled and diced
- 1 small jalapeño pepper, diced
- ½ red bell pepper, diced
- ½ red onion, minced
- Pinch chopped fresh cilantro
- Juice of ½ lime
- ¼ teaspoon salt
- ¼ teaspoon ground black pepper
- 120 ml Mexican beer
- 1 egg
- 75 g cornflour
- 90 g plain flour
- ½ teaspoon ground cumin
- ¼ teaspoon chilli powder
- 455 g cod, cut into 4 pieces
- Olive oil spray
- 4 corn tortillas, or flour tortillas, at room temperature

DIRECTIONS
1. In a small bowl, stir together the mango, jalapeño, red bell pepper, red onion, cilantro, lime juice, salt, and pepper. Set aside.
2. In a medium bowl, whisk the beer and egg.
3. In another medium bowl, stir together the cornflour, flour, cumin, and chilli powder.
4. Insert the crisper plate into the basket and the basket into the unit. Preheat the unit to 192ºC.
5. Dip the fish pieces into the egg mixture and in the flour mixture to coat completely.
6. Once the unit is preheated, place a baking paper liner into the basket. Place the fish on the liner in a single layer.
7. Cook for about 9 minutes, spray the fish with olive oil. Reinsert the basket to resume cooking.
8. When the cooking is complete, the fish should be golden and crispy. Place the pieces in the tortillas, top with the mango salsa, and serve.

Chapter 6 Vegetables and Sides

Saltine Wax Beans

Serves 4
Cook time: 7 minutes

INGREDIENTS

- 60 g flour
- 1 teaspoon smoky chipotle powder
- ½ teaspoon ground black pepper
- 1 teaspoon sea salt flakes
- 2 eggs, beaten
- 55 g crushed cream crackers
- 285 g wax beans
- Cooking spray

DIRECTIONS

1. Preheat the air fryer to 180ºC.
2. Combine the flour, chipotle powder, black pepper, and salt in a bowl. Put the eggs in a second bowl. Put the crushed cream crackers in a third bowl.
3. Wash the beans with cold water and discard any tough strings.
4. Coat the beans with the flour mixture, before dipping them into the beaten egg. Cover them with the crushed cream crackers.
5. Spritz the beans with cooking spray.
6. Air fry for 4 minutes. Give the air fryer basket a good shake and continue to air fry for 3 minutes. Serve hot.

Marinara Pepperoni Mushroom Pizza

Serves 4
Cook time: 18 minutes

INGREDIENTS

- 4 large portobello mushrooms, stems removed
- 4 teaspoons olive oil
- 225 g marinara sauce
- 225 g shredded Mozzarella cheese
- 10 slices sugar-free pepperoni

DIRECTIONS

1. Preheat the air fryer to 192ºC.

2. Brush each mushroom cap with the olive oil, one teaspoon for each cap.
3. Put on a baking sheet and bake, stem-side down, for 8 minutes.
4. Take out of the air fryer and divide the marinara sauce, Mozzarella cheese and pepperoni evenly among the caps.
5. Air fry for another 10 minutes until browned.
6. Serve hot.

Golden Garlicky Mushrooms

Serves 4
Cook time: 10 minutes

INGREDIENTS

- 6 small mushrooms
- 1 tablespoon bread crumbs
- 1 tablespoon olive oil
- 30 g onion, peeled and diced
- 1 teaspoon parsley
- 1 teaspoon garlic purée
- Salt and ground black pepper, to taste

DIRECTIONS

1. Preheat the air fryer to 180°C.
2. Combine the bread crumbs, oil, onion, parsley, salt, pepper and garlic in a bowl. Cut out the mushrooms' stalks and stuff each cap with the crumb mixture.
3. Air fry in the air fryer for 10 minutes.
4. Serve hot.

Cheese-Walnut Stuffed Mushrooms

Serves 4
Cook time: 10 minutes

INGREDIENTS

- 4 large portobello mushrooms
- 1 tablespoon rapeseed oil
- 110 g shredded Mozzarella cheese
- 35 g minced walnuts
- 2 tablespoons chopped fresh parsley
- Cooking spray

DIRECTIONS

1. Preheat the air fryer to 180°C. Spritz the air fryer basket with cooking spray.

2. On a clean work surface, remove the mushroom stems. Scoop out the gills with a spoon and discard. Coat the mushrooms with rapeseed oil. Top each mushroom evenly with the shredded Mozzarella cheese, followed by the minced walnuts.

3. Arrange the mushrooms in the air fryer and roast for 10 minutes until golden brown.

4. Transfer the mushrooms to a plate and sprinkle the parsley on top for garnish before serving.

Roasted Potatoes and Asparagus

Serves 4
Cook time: 23 minutes

INGREDIENTS

- 4 medium potatoes
- 1 bunch asparagus
- 75 g cottage cheese
- 80 g low-fat crème fraiche
- 1 tablespoon wholegrain mustard
- Salt and pepper, to taste
- Cooking spray

DIRECTIONS

1. Preheat the air fryer to 200ºC. Spritz the air fryer basket with cooking spray.

2. Place the potatoes in the basket. Air fry the potatoes for 20 minutes.

3. Boil the asparagus in salted water for 3 minutes.

4. Remove the potatoes and mash them with rest of ingredients. Sprinkle with salt and pepper.

5. Serve immediately.

Sesame Taj Tofu

Serves 4
Cook time: 25 minutes

INGREDIENTS

- 1 block firm tofu, pressed and cut into 1-inch thick cubes
- 2 tablespoons soy sauce
- 2 teaspoons toasted sesame seeds
- 1 teaspoon rice vinegar
- 1 tablespoon cornflour

DIRECTIONS

1. Preheat the air fryer to 200ºC.

2. Add the tofu, soy sauce, sesame seeds, and rice vinegar in a bowl together and mix well to coat the tofu cubes. Then cover the tofu in cornflour and put it in the air fryer basket.

3. Air fry for 25 minutes, giving the basket a shake at five-minute intervals to ensure the tofu cooks evenly.
4. Serve immediately.

Air Fried Potatoes with Olives

Serves 1
Cook time: 40 minutes

INGREDIENTS

- 1 medium Maris Piper potatoes, scrubbed and peeled
- 1 teaspoon olive oil
- ¼ teaspoon onion powder
- ⅛ teaspoon salt
- Dollop of butter
- Dollop of cream cheese
- 1 tablespoon Kalamata olives
- 1 tablespoon chopped chives

DIRECTIONS

1. Preheat the air fryer to 200ºC.
2. In a bowl, coat the potatoes with the onion powder, salt, olive oil, and butter.
3. Transfer to the air fryer and air fry for 40 minutes, turning the potatoes over at the halfway point.
4. Take care when removing the potatoes from the air fryer and serve with the cream cheese, Kalamata olives and chives on top.

Lush Vegetable Salad

Serves 4
Cook time: 10 minutes

INGREDIENTS

- 6 plum tomatoes, halved
- 2 large red onions, sliced
- 4 long red pepper, sliced
- 2 yellow pepper, sliced
- 6 cloves garlic, crushed
- 1 tablespoon extra-virgin olive oil
- 1 teaspoon paprika
- ½ lemon, juiced
- Salt and ground black pepper, to taste
- 1 tablespoon baby capers

DIRECTIONS

1. Preheat the air fryer to 220ºC.
2. Put the tomatoes, onions, peppers, and garlic in a large bowl and cover with the extra-virgin olive oil, paprika, and lemon juice. Sprinkle with salt and pepper as desired.
3. Line the inside of the air fryer basket with aluminum foil. Put the vegetables inside and air fry for 10 minutes, ensuring the edges turn brown.
4. Serve in a salad bowl with the baby capers.

Fig, Chickpea, and Rocket Salad

Serves 4
Cook time: 20 minutes

INGREDIENTS

- 8 fresh figs, halved
- 250 g cooked chickpeas
- 1 teaspoon crushed roasted cumin seeds
- 4 tablespoons balsamic vinegar
- 2 tablespoons extra-virgin olive oil, plus more for greasing
- Salt and ground black pepper, to taste
- 40 g rocket, washed and dried

DIRECTIONS

1. Preheat the air fryer to 192ºC.
2. Cover the air fryer basket with aluminum foil and grease lightly with oil. Put the figs in the air fryer basket and air fry for 10 minutes.
3. In a bowl, combine the chickpeas and cumin seeds.
4. Remove the air fried figs from the air fryer and replace with the chickpeas. Air fry for 10 minutes. Leave to cool.
5. In the meantime, prepare the dressing. Mix the balsamic vinegar, olive oil, salt and pepper.
6. In a salad bowl, combine the rocket with the cooled figs and chickpeas.
7. Toss with the sauce and serve.

Gorgonzola Mushrooms with Horseradish Mayo

Serves 5
Cook time: 10 minutes

INGREDIENTS

- 60 g bread crumbs
- 2 cloves garlic, pressed
- 2 tablespoons chopped fresh coriander
- ⅓ teaspoon coarse sea salt

- ½ teaspoon crushed red pepper flakes
- 1½ tablespoons olive oil
- 20 medium mushrooms, stems removed
- 55 g grated Gorgonzola cheese
- 55 g low-fat mayonnaise
- 1 teaspoon prepared horseradish, well-drained
- 1 tablespoon finely chopped fresh parsley

DIRECTIONS

1. Preheat the air fryer to 192ºC.
2. Combine the bread crumbs together with the garlic, coriander, salt, red pepper, and olive oil.
3. Take equal-sized amounts of the bread crumb mixture and use them to stuff the mushroom caps. Add the grated Gorgonzola on top of each.
4. Put the mushrooms in a baking pan and transfer to the air fryer.
5. Air fry for 10 minutes, ensuring the stuffing is warm throughout.
6. In the meantime, prepare the horseradish mayo. Mix the mayonnaise, horseradish and parsley.
7. When the mushrooms are ready, serve with the mayo.

Ricotta Potatoes

Serves 4
Cook time: 15 minutes

INGREDIENTS

- 4 potatoes
- 2 tablespoons olive oil
- 110 g Ricotta cheese, at room temperature
- 2 tablespoons chopped spring onions
- 1 tablespoon roughly chopped fresh parsley
- 1 tablespoon minced coriander
- 60 g Cheddar cheese, preferably freshly grated
- 1 teaspoon celery seeds
- ½ teaspoon salt
- ½ teaspoon garlic pepper

DIRECTIONS

1. Preheat the air fryer to 180ºC.
2. Pierce the skin of the potatoes with a knife.
3. Air fry in the air fryer basket for 13 minutes. If they are not cooked through by this time, leave for 2 to 3 minutes longer.
4. In the meantime, make the stuffing by combining all the other ingredients.
5. Cut halfway into the cooked potatoes to open them.
6. Spoon equal amounts of the stuffing into each potato and serve hot.

Tamarind Sweet Potatoes

Serves 4

Cook time: 20 to 25 minutes

INGREDIENTS

- 5 garnet sweet potatoes, peeled and diced
- 1½ tablespoons fresh lime juice
- 1 tablespoon butter, melted
- 2 teaspoons tamarind paste
- 1½ teaspoon ground allspice
- ⅓ teaspoon white pepper
- ½ teaspoon turmeric powder
- A few drops liquid stevia

DIRECTIONS

1. Preheat the air fryer to 200ºC.
2. In a large mixing bowl, combine all the ingredients and toss until the sweet potatoes are evenly coated.
3. Place the sweet potatoes in the air fryer basket and air fry for 20 t0 25 minutes, or until the potatoes are crispy on the outside and soft on the inside. Shake the basket twice during cooking.
4. Let the potatoes cool for 5 minutes before serving.

Scalloped Potatoes

Serves 4

Cook time: 20 minutes

INGREDIENTS

- 440 g sliced frozen potatoes, thawed
- 3 cloves garlic, minced
- Pinch salt
- Freshly ground black pepper, to taste
- 180 g double cream

DIRECTIONS

1. Preheat the air fryer to 192ºC.
2. Toss the potatoes with the garlic, salt, and black pepper in a baking pan until evenly coated. Pour the double cream over the top.
3. Place the baking pan in the air fryer basket and bake for 15 minutes, or until the potatoes are tender and top is golden brown. Check for doneness and bake for another 5 minutes as needed.
4. Serve hot.

Citrus Sweet Potatoes and Carrots

Serves 4

Cook time: 20 to 25 minutes

INGREDIENTS

- 2 large carrots, cut into 1-inch chunks
- 1 medium sweet potato, peeled and cut into 1-inch cubes
- 25 g chopped onion
- 2 garlic cloves, minced
- 2 tablespoons honey
- 1 tablespoon freshly squeezed orange juice
- 2 teaspoons butter, melted

DIRECTIONS

1. Insert the crisper plate into the basket and the basket into the unit. Preheat the unit by selecting AIR ROAST, setting the temperature to 200ºC, and setting the time to 3 minutes. Select START/STOP to begin.
2. In a 6-by-2-inch round pan, toss together the carrots, sweet potato, onion, garlic, honey, orange juice, and melted butter to coat.
3. Once the unit is preheated, place the pan into the basket.
4. Select AIR ROAST, set the temperature to 200ºC, and set the time to 25 minutes. Select START/STOP to begin.
5. After 15 minutes, remove the basket and shake the vegetables. Reinsert the basket to resume cooking. After 5 minutes, if the vegetables are tender and glazed, they are done. If not, resume cooking.
6. When the cooking is complete, serve immediately.

Chapter 7 Desserts

Bourbon Bread Pudding

Serves 4
Cook time: 20 minutes

INGREDIENTS

- 3 slices whole grain bread, cubed
- 1 large egg
- 240 ml whole milk
- 2 tablespoons bourbon, or peach juice
- ½ teaspoons vanilla extract
- 4 tablespoons maple syrup, divided
- ½ teaspoons ground cinnamon
- 2 teaspoons sparkling sugar

DIRECTIONS

1. Preheat the air fryer to 132ºC.
2. Spray a baking pan with nonstick cooking spray, then place the bread cubes in the pan.
3. In a medium bowl, whisk together the egg, milk, bourbon, vanilla extract, 3 tablespoons of maple syrup, and cinnamon. Pour the egg mixture over the bread and press down with a spatula to coat all the bread, then sprinkle the sparkling sugar on top and bake for 20 minutes.
4. Remove the pudding from the air fryer and allow to cool in the pan on a wire rack for 10 minutes. Drizzle the remaining 1 tablespoon of maple syrup on top. Slice and serve warm.

Apple Wedges with Apricots

Serves 4
Cook time: 15 to 18 minutes

INGREDIENTS

- 4 large apples, peeled and sliced into 8 wedges
- 2 tablespoons light olive oil
- 95 g dried apricots, chopped
- 1 to 2 tablespoons granulated sugar
- ½ teaspoon ground cinnamon

DIRECTIONS

1. Preheat the air fryer to 180ºC.
2. Toss the apple wedges with the olive oil in a mixing bowl until well coated.
3. Place the apple wedges in the air fryer basket and air fry for 12 to 15 minutes.

4. Sprinkle with the dried apricots and air fry for another 3 minutes.
5. Meanwhile, thoroughly combine the sugar and cinnamon in a small bowl.
6. Remove the apple wedges from the basket to a plate. Serve sprinkled with the sugar mixture.

Pecan and Cherry Stuffed Apples

Serves 4
Cook time: 20 minutes

INGREDIENTS

- 4 apples (about 565 g)
- 40 g chopped pecans
- 50 g dried tart cherries
- 1 tablespoon melted butter
- 3 tablespoons brown sugar
- ¼ teaspoon allspice
- Pinch salt
- Ice cream, for serving

DIRECTIONS

1. Cut off top ½ inch from each apple; reserve tops. With a melon baller, core through stem ends without breaking through the bottom. (Do not trim bases.)
2. Preheat the air fryer to 176ºC. Combine pecans, cherries, butter, brown sugar, allspice, and a pinch of salt. Stuff mixture into the hollow centers of the apples. Cover with apple tops. Put in the air fryer basket, using tongs. Air fry for 20 to 25 minutes, or just until tender.
3. Serve warm with ice cream.

Cinnamon and Pecan Pie

Serves 4
Cook time: 25 minutes

INGREDIENTS

- 1 pack shortcrust pastry
- ½ teaspoons cinnamon
- ¾ teaspoon vanilla extract
- 2 eggs
- 175 ml maple syrup
- ⅛ teaspoon nutmeg
- 3 tablespoons melted butter, divided
- 2 tablespoons sugar
- 65 g chopped pecans

DIRECTIONS

1. Preheat the air fryer to 188°C.
2. In a small bowl, coat the pecans in 1 tablespoon of melted butter.
3. Transfer the pecans to the air fryer and air fry for about 10 minutes.
4. Put the pie dough in a greased pie pan, trim off the excess and add the pecans on top.
5. In a bowl, mix the rest of the ingredients. Pour this over the pecans.
6. Put the pan in the air fryer and bake for 25 minutes.
7. Serve immediately.

Baked Peaches with Yogurt and Blueberries

Serves 6
Cook time: 7 to 11 minutes

INGREDIENTS

- 3 peaches, peeled, halved, and pitted
- 2 tablespoons packed brown sugar
- 285 g plain Greek yogurt
- ¼ teaspoon ground cinnamon
- 1 teaspoon pure vanilla extract
- 190 g fresh blueberries

DIRECTIONS

1. Preheat the air fryer to 192°C.
2. Arrange the peaches in the air fryer basket, cut side up. Top with a generous sprinkle of brown sugar.
3. Bake in the preheated air fryer for 7 to 11 minutes, or until the peaches are lightly browned and caramelized.
4. Meanwhile, whisk together the yogurt, cinnamon, and vanilla in a small bowl until smooth.
5. Remove the peaches from the basket to a plate. Serve topped with the yogurt mixture and fresh blueberries.

Vanilla and Cardamon Walnuts Tart

Serves 6
Cook time: 13 minutes

INGREDIENTS

- 240 ml coconut milk
- 60 g walnuts, ground
- 60 g powdered sweetener
- 55 g almond flour

- 55 g butter, at room temperature
- 2 eggs
- 1 teaspoon vanilla essence
- ¼ teaspoon ground cardamom
- ¼ teaspoon ground cloves
- Cooking spray

DIRECTIONS

1. Preheat the air fryer to 184ºC. Coat a baking pan with cooking spray.
2. Combine all the ingredients except the oil in a large bowl and stir until well blended. Spoon the batter mixture into the baking pan.
3. Bake in the preheated air fryer for approximately 13 minutes. Check the tart for doneness: If a toothpick inserted into the center of the tart comes out clean, it's done.
4. Remove from the air fryer and place on a wire rack to cool. Serve immediately.

Simple Pineapple Sticks

Serves 4
Cook time: 10 minutes

INGREDIENTS

- ½ fresh pineapple, cut into sticks
- 25 g desiccated coconut

DIRECTIONS

1. Preheat the air fryer to 204ºC.
2. Coat the pineapple sticks in the desiccated coconut and put each one in the air fryer basket.
3. Air fry for 10 minutes.
4. Serve immediately

Crispy Pineapple Rings

Serves 6
Cook time: 6 to 8 minutes

INGREDIENTS

- 240 ml rice milk
- 85 g plain flour
- 120 ml water
- 25 g unsweetened flaked coconut
- 4 tablespoons granulated sugar
- ½ teaspoon baking soda

- ½ teaspoon baking powder
- ½ teaspoon vanilla essence
- ½ teaspoon ground cinnamon
- ¼ teaspoon ground star anise
- Pinch of kosher, or coarse sea salt
- 1 medium pineapple, peeled and sliced

DIRECTIONS

1. Preheat the air fryer to 192°C.
2. In a large bowl, stir together all the ingredients except the pineapple.
3. Dip each pineapple slice into the batter until evenly coated.
4. Arrange the pineapple slices in the basket and air fry for 6 to 8 minutes until golden brown.
5. Remove from the basket to a plate and cool for 5 minutes before serving warm

Caramelized Fruit Skewers

Serves 4
Cook time: 3 to 5 minutes

INGREDIENTS

- 2 peaches, peeled, pitted, and thickly sliced
- 3 plums, halved and pitted
- 3 nectarines, halved and pitted
- 1 tablespoon honey
- ½ teaspoon ground cinnamon
- ¼ teaspoon ground allspice
- Pinch cayenne pepper
- Special Equipment:
- 8 metal skewers

DIRECTIONS

1. Preheat the air fryer to 204°C.
2. Thread, alternating peaches, plums, and nectarines, onto the metal skewers that fit into the air fryer.
3. Thoroughly combine the honey, cinnamon, allspice, and cayenne in a small bowl. Brush the glaze generously over the fruit skewers.
4. Transfer the fruit skewers to the air fryer basket. You may need to cook in batches to avoid overcrowding.
5. Air fry for 3 to 5 minutes, or until the fruit is caramelized.
6. Remove from the basket and repeat with the remaining fruit skewers.
7. Let the fruit skewers rest for 5 minutes before serving.

Pumpkin Pudding with Vanilla Wafers

Serves 4
Cook time: 12 to 17 minutes

INGREDIENTS

- 250 g canned no-salt-added pumpkin purée (not pumpkin pie filling)
- 50 g packed brown sugar
- 3 tablespoons plain flour
- 1 egg, whisked
- 2 tablespoons milk
- 1 tablespoon unsalted butter, melted
- 1 teaspoon pure vanilla extract
- 4 low-fat vanilla, or plain wafers, crumbled
- Nonstick cooking spray

DIRECTIONS

1. Preheat the air fryer to 176°C. Coat a baking pan with nonstick cooking spray. Set aside.
2. Mix the pumpkin purée, brown sugar, flour, whisked egg, milk, melted butter, and vanilla in a medium bowl and whisk to combine. Transfer the mixture to the baking pan.
3. Place the baking pan in the air fryer basket and bake for 12 to 17 minutes until set.
4. Remove the pudding from the basket to a wire rack to cool.
5. Divide the pudding into four bowls and serve with the vanilla wafers sprinkled on top.

Blackberry Peach Cobbler with Vanilla

Serves 4
Cook time: 20 minutes

INGREDIENTS
Filling:

- 170 g blackberries
- 250 g chopped peaches, cut into ½-inch thick slices
- 2 teaspoons arrowroot or cornflour
- 2 tablespoons coconut sugar
- 1 teaspoon lemon juice

Topping:

- 2 tablespoons sunflower oil
- 1 tablespoon maple syrup
- 1 teaspoon vanilla
- 3 tablespoons coconut sugar
- 40 g rolled oats

- 45 g whole-wheat pastry, or plain flour
- 1 teaspoon cinnamon
- ¼ teaspoon nutmeg
- ⅛ teaspoon sea salt

DIRECTIONS
Make the Filling:
1. Combine the blackberries, peaches, arrowroot, coconut sugar, and lemon juice in a baking pan.
2. Using a rubber spatula, stir until well incorporated. Set aside. Make the Topping:
3. Preheat the air fryer to 162°C
4. Combine the oil, maple syrup, and vanilla in a mixing bowl and stir well. Whisk in the remaining ingredients. Spread this mixture evenly over the filling.
5. Place the pan in the air fryer basket and bake for 20 minutes, or until the topping is crispy and golden brown. Serve warm

Breaded Bananas with Chocolate Topping

Serves 6
Cook time: 10 minutes

INGREDIENTS
- 40 g cornflour
- 25 g plain breadcrumbs
- 1 large egg, beaten
- 3 bananas, halved crosswise
- Cooking spray
- Chocolate sauce, for serving

DIRECTIONS
1. Preheat the air fryer to176°C.
2. Place the cornflour, breadcrumbs, and egg in three separate bowls.
3. Roll the bananas in the cornstarch, then in the beaten egg, and finally in the breadcrumbs to coat well.
4. Spritz the air fryer basket with the cooking spray.
5. Arrange the banana halves in the basket and mist them with the cooking spray. Air fry for 5 minutes. Flip the bananas and continue to air fry for another 2 minutes.
6. Remove the bananas from the basket to a serving plate. Serve with the chocolate sauce drizzled over the top.

Coconut Mixed Berry Crisp

Serves 6
Cook time: 20 minutes

INGREDIENTS

- 1 tablespoon butter, melted
- 340 g mixed berries
- 65 g granulated sweetener
- 1 teaspoon pure vanilla extract
- ½ teaspoon ground cinnamon
- ¼ teaspoon ground cloves
- ¼ teaspoon grated nutmeg
- 50 g coconut chips, for garnish

DIRECTIONS

1. Preheat the air fryer to 164°C. Coat a baking pan with melted butter.
2. Put the remaining ingredients except the coconut chips in the prepared baking pan.
3. Bake in the preheated air fryer for 20 minutes.
4. Serve garnished with the coconut chips.

Chocolate and Rum Cupcakes

Serves 6
Cook time: 15 minutes

INGREDIENTS

- 150 g granulated sweetener
- 140 g almond flour
- 1 teaspoon unsweetened baking powder
- 3 teaspoons cocoa powder
- ½ teaspoon baking soda
- ½ teaspoon ground cinnamon
- ¼ teaspoon grated nutmeg
- ⅛ teaspoon salt
- 120 ml milk
- 110 g butter, at room temperature
- 3 eggs, whisked
- 1 teaspoon pure rum extract
- 70 g blueberries
- Cooking spray

DIRECTIONS

1. Preheat the air fryer to 176°C. Spray a 6-cup muffin tin with cooking spray.
2. In a mixing bowl, combine the sweetener, almond flour, baking powder, cocoa powder, baking soda, cinnamon, nutmeg, and salt and stir until well blended.
3. In another mixing bowl, mix together the milk, butter, egg, and rum extract until thoroughly combined. Slowly and carefully pour this mixture into the bowl of dry mixture. Stir in the

blueberries.

4. Spoon the batter into the greased muffin cups, filling each about three-quarters full.
5. Bake for 15 minutes, or until the center is springy and a toothpick inserted in the middle comes out clean.
6. Remove from the basket and place on a wire rack to cool. Serve immediately.

Mixed Berries with Pecan Streusel Topping

Serves 3
Cook time: 17 minutes

INGREDIENTS

- 75 g mixed berries
- Cooking spray

Topping:

- 1 egg, beaten
- 3 tablespoons almonds, slivered
- 3 tablespoons chopped pecans
- 2 tablespoons chopped walnuts
- 3 tablespoons granulated sweetener
- 2 tablespoons cold salted butter, cut into pieces
- ½ teaspoon ground cinnamon

DIRECTIONS

1. Preheat the air fryer to 172°C. Lightly spray a baking dish with cooking spray.
2. Make the topping: In a medium bowl, stir together the beaten egg, nuts, sweetener, butter, and cinnamon until well blended.
3. Put the mixed berries in the bottom of the baking dish and spread the topping over the top.
4. Bake in the preheated air fryer for 17 minutes, or until the fruit is bubbly and topping is golden brown.
5. Allow to cool for 5 to 10 minutes before serving.

Air Fryer Apple Fritters

Serves 6
Cook time: 7 to 8 minutes

INGREDIENTS

- 1 chopped, peeled Granny Smith apple
- 115 g granulated sugar
- 1 teaspoon ground cinnamon
- 120 g plain flour
- 1 teaspoon baking powder

- 1 teaspoon salt
- 2 tablespoons milk
- 2 tablespoons butter, melted
- 1 large egg, beaten
- Cooking spray
- 25 g icing sugar (optional)

DIRECTIONS

1. Mix together the apple, granulated sugar, and cinnamon in a small bowl. Allow to sit for 30 minutes.
2. Combine the flour, baking powder, and salt in a medium bowl. Add the milk, butter, and egg and stir to incorporate.
3. Pour the apple mixture into the bowl of flour mixture and stir with a spatula until a dough forms.
4. Make the fritters: On a clean work surface, divide the dough into 12 equal portions and shape into 1-inch balls. Flatten them into patties with your hands.
5. Preheat the air fryer to 176ºC. Line the air fryer basket with baking paper and spray it with cooking spray.
6. Transfer the apple fritters onto the baking paper, evenly spaced but not too close together. Spray the fritters with cooking spray.
7. Bake for 7 to 8 minutes until lightly browned. Flip the fritters halfway through the cooking time.
8. Remove from the basket to a plate and serve with the confectioners' sugar sprinkled on top, if desired.

Chapter 8 Snacks and Appetizers

Root Veggie Chips with Herb Salt

Serves 2
Cook time: 8 minutes

INGREDIENTS

- 1 parsnip, washed
- 1 small beetroot, washed
- 1 small turnip, washed
- ½ small sweet potato, washed
- 1 teaspoon olive oil
- Cooking spray
- Herb Salt:
- ¼ teaspoon rock salt
- 2 teaspoons finely chopped fresh parsley

DIRECTIONS

1. Preheat the air fryer to 182ºC.
2. Peel and thinly slice the parsnip, beetroot, turnip, and sweet potato, then place the vegetables in a large bowl, add the olive oil, and toss.
3. Spray the air fryer basket with cooking spray, then place the vegetables in the basket and air fry for 8 minutes, gently shaking the basket halfway through.
4. While the chips cook, make the herb salt in a small bowl by combining the rock salt and parsley.
5. Remove the chips and place on a serving plate, then sprinkle the herb salt on top and allow to cool for 2 to 3 minutes before serving.

Sausage Balls with Cheese

Serves 8
Cook time: 10 to 11 minutes

INGREDIENTS

- 340 g mild sausage meat
- 355 ml baking mix
- 240 ml shredded mild Cheddar cheese
- 85 g soft white cheese, at room temperature
- 1 to 2 tablespoons olive oil

DIRECTIONS

1. Preheat the air fryer to 164ºC. Line the air fryer basket with parchment paper.

2. Mix together the ground sausage, baking mix, Cheddar cheese, and soft white cheese in a large bowl and stir to incorporate.

3. Divide the sausage mixture into 16 equal portions and roll them into 1-inch balls with your hands.

4. Arrange the sausage balls on the parchment, leaving space between each ball. You may need to work in batches to avoid overcrowding.

5. Brush the sausage balls with the olive oil. Bake for 10 to 11 minutes, shaking the basket halfway through, or until the balls are firm and lightly browned on both sides.

6. Remove from the basket to a plate and repeat with the remaining balls.

7. Serve warm.

Cheesy Courgette Tots

Serves 8
Cook time: 6 minutes

INGREDIENTS

- 2 medium courgette (about 340 g), shredded
- 1 large egg, whisked
- 120 ml grated pecorino Romano cheese
- 120 ml panko breadcrumbs
- ¼ teaspoon black pepper
- 1 clove garlic, minced
- Cooking spray

DIRECTIONS

1. Using your hands, squeeze out as much liquid from the courgette as possible. In a large bowl, mix the courgette with the remaining ingredients except the oil until well incorporated.

2. Make the courgette tots: Use a spoon or cookie scoop to place tablespoonfuls of the courgette mixture onto a lightly floured cutting board and form into 1-inch logs.

3. Preheat air fryer to 192°C. Spritz the air fryer basket with cooking spray.

4. Place the tots in the basket. You may need to cook in batches to avoid overcrowding.

5. Air fry for 6 minutes until golden brown.

6. Remove from the basket to a serving plate and repeat with the remaining courgette tots.

7. Serve immediately.

Browned Ricotta with Capers and Lemon

Serves 4 to 6
Cook time: 8 to 10 minutes

INGREDIENTS

- 355 ml whole milk ricotta cheese

- 2 tablespoons extra-virgin olive oil
- 2 tablespoons capers, rinsed
- Zest of 1 lemon, plus more for garnish
- 1 teaspoon finely chopped fresh rosemary
- Pinch crushed red pepper flakes
- Salt and freshly ground black pepper, to taste
- 1 tablespoon grated Parmesan cheese

DIRECTIONS

1. Preheat the air fryer to 192°C.
2. In a mixing bowl, stir together the ricotta cheese, olive oil, capers, lemon zest, rosemary, red pepper flakes, salt, and pepper until well combined.
3. Spread the mixture evenly in a baking dish and place it in the air fryer basket.
4. Air fry for 8 to 10 minutes until the top is nicely browned.
5. Remove from the basket and top with a sprinkle of grated Parmesan cheese.
6. Garnish with the lemon zest and serve warm.

Hush Puppies

Serves 12
Cook time: 10 minutes

INGREDIENTS

- 240 ml self-raising yellow cornmeal
- 120 ml plain flour
- 1 teaspoon sugar
- 1 teaspoon salt
- 1 teaspoon freshly ground black pepper
- 1 large egg
- 80 ml canned creamed corn
- 240 ml minced onion
- 2 teaspoons minced jalapeño pepper
- 2 tablespoons olive oil, divided

DIRECTIONS

1. Thoroughly combine the cornmeal, flour, sugar, salt, and pepper in a large bowl.
2. Whisk together the egg and corn in a small bowl. Pour the egg mixture into the bowl of cornmeal mixture and stir to combine. Stir in the minced onion and jalapeño. Cover the bowl with plastic wrap and place in the refrigerator for 30 minutes.
3. Preheat the air fryer to 192°C. Line the air fryer basket with parchment paper and lightly brush it with 1 tablespoon of olive oil.
4. Scoop out the cornmeal mixture and form into 24 balls, about 1 inch.
5. Arrange the balls in the parchment paper-lined basket, leaving space between each ball.

6. Air fry in batches for 5 minutes. Shake the basket and brush the balls with the remaining 1 tablespoon of olive oil. Continue cooking for 5 minutes until golden brown.

7. Remove the balls (hush puppies) from the basket and serve on a plate.

Shrimp Toasts with Sesame Seeds

Serves 4 to 6
Cook time: 6 to 8 minutes

INGREDIENTS

- 230 g raw shrimp, peeled and deveined
- 1 egg, beaten
- 2 spring onions, chopped, plus more for garnish
- 2 tablespoons chopped fresh coriander
- 2 teaspoons grated fresh ginger
- 1 to 2 teaspoons sriracha sauce
- 1 teaspoon soy sauce
- ½ teaspoon toasted sesame oil
- 6 slices thinly sliced white sandwich bread
- 120 ml sesame seeds
- Cooking spray
- Thai chilli sauce, for serving

DIRECTIONS

1. Preheat the air fryer to 204°C. Spritz the air fryer basket with cooking spray.

2. In a food processor, add the shrimp, egg, spring onions, coriander, ginger, sriracha sauce, soy sauce and sesame oil, and pulse until chopped finely. You'll need to stop the food processor occasionally to scrape down the sides. Transfer the shrimp mixture to a bowl.

3. On a clean work surface, cut the crusts off the sandwich bread. Using a brush, generously brush one side of each slice of bread with shrimp mixture.

4. Place the sesame seeds on a plate. Press bread slices, shrimp-side down, into sesame seeds to coat evenly. Cut each slice diagonally into quarters.

5. Spread the coated slices in a single layer in the air fryer basket.

6. Air fry in batches for 6 to 8 minutes, or until golden and crispy. Flip the bread slices halfway through. Repeat with the remaining bread slices.

7. Transfer to a plate and let cool for 5 minutes. Top with the chopped spring onions and serve warm with Thai chilli sauce.

Tangy Fried Pickle Spears

Serves 6
Cook time: 15 minutes

INGREDIENTS

- 2 jars sweet and sour pickle spears, patted dry
- 2 medium-sized eggs
- 80 ml milk
- 1 teaspoon garlic powder
- 1 teaspoon sea salt
- ½ teaspoon shallot powder
- ⅓ teaspoon chilli powder
- 80 ml plain flour
- Cooking spray

DIRECTIONS

1. Preheat the air fryer to 196°C. Spritz the air fryer basket with cooking spray.
2. In a bowl, beat together the eggs with milk. In another bowl, combine garlic powder, sea salt, shallot powder, chilli powder and plain flour until well blended.
3. One by one, roll the pickle spears in the powder mixture, then dredge them in the egg mixture. Dip them in the powder mixture a second time for additional coating.
4. Arrange the coated pickles in the prepared basket. Air fry for 15 minutes until golden and crispy, shaking the basket halfway through to ensure even cooking.
5. Transfer to a plate and let cool for 5 minutes before serving.

Old Bay Chicken Wings

Serves 4
Cook time: 12 to 15 minutes

INGREDIENTS

- 2 tablespoons Old Bay or all-purpose seasoning
- 2 teaspoons baking powder
- 2 teaspoons salt
- 900 g chicken wings, patted dry
- Cooking spray

DIRECTIONS

1. Preheat the air fryer to 204°C. Lightly spray the air fryer basket with cooking spray.
2. Combine the seasoning, baking powder, and salt in a large zip-top plastic bag. Add the chicken wings, seal, and shake until the wings are thoroughly coated in the seasoning mixture.
3. Lay the chicken wings in the air fryer basket in a single layer and lightly mist with cooking spray. You may need to work in batches to avoid overcrowding.
4. Air fry for 12 to 15 minutes, flipping the wings halfway through, or until the wings are lightly browned and the internal temperature reaches at least 74°C on a meat thermometer.
5. Remove from the basket to a plate and repeat with the remaining chicken wings.
6. Serve hot.

Crispy Green Tomatoes with Horseradish

Serves 4
Cook time: 10 to 15 minutes

INGREDIENTS

- 2 eggs
- 60 ml buttermilk
- 120 ml breadcrumbs
- 120 ml cornmeal
- ¼ teaspoon salt
- 680 g firm green tomatoes, cut into ¼-inch slices
- Cooking spray
- Horseradish Sauce:
- 60 ml sour cream
- 60 ml mayonnaise
- 2 teaspoons prepared horseradish
- ½ teaspoon lemon juice
- ½ teaspoon Worcestershire sauce
- ⅛ teaspoon black pepper

DIRECTIONS

1. Preheat air fryer to 200ºC. Spritz the air fryer basket with cooking spray.
2. In a small bowl, whisk together all the ingredients for the horseradish sauce until smooth. Set aside.
3. In a shallow dish, beat the eggs and buttermilk.
4. In a separate shallow dish, thoroughly combine the breadcrumbs, cornmeal, and salt.
5. Dredge the tomato slices, one at a time, in the egg mixture, then roll in the bread crumb mixture until evenly coated.
6. Working in batches, place the tomato slices in the air fryer basket in a single layer. Spray them with cooking spray.
7. Air fry for 10 to 15 minutes, flipping the slices halfway through, or until the tomato slices are nicely browned and crisp.
8. Remove from the basket to a platter and repeat with the remaining tomato slices.
9. Serve drizzled with the prepared horseradish sauce.

Italian Rice Balls

Makes 8 rice balls
Cook time: 10 minutes

INGREDIENTS

- 355 ml cooked sticky rice

- ½ teaspoon Italian seasoning blend
- ¾ teaspoon salt, divided
- 8 black olives, pitted
- 28 g Mozzarella cheese, cut into tiny pieces (small enough to stuff into olives)
- 2 eggs
- 80 ml Italian breadcrumbs
- 177 ml panko breadcrumbs
- Cooking spray

DIRECTIONS

1. Preheat air fryer to 200°C.
2. Stuff each black olive with a piece of Mozzarella cheese. Set aside.
3. In a bowl, combine the cooked sticky rice, Italian seasoning blend, and ½ teaspoon of salt and stir to mix well. Form the rice mixture into a log with your hands and divide it into 8 equal portions. Mould each portion around a black olive and roll into a ball.
4. Transfer to the freezer to chill for 10 to 15 minutes until firm.
5. In a shallow dish, place the Italian breadcrumbs. In a separate shallow dish, whisk the eggs. In a third shallow dish, combine the panko breadcrumbs and remaining salt.
6. One by one, roll the rice balls in the Italian breadcrumbs, then dip in the whisked eggs, finally coat them with the panko breadcrumbs.
7. Arrange the rice balls in the air fryer basket and spritz both sides with cooking spray.
8. Air fry for 10 minutes until the rice balls are golden brown. Flip the balls halfway through the cooking time.
9. Serve warm.

Pork and Cabbage Egg Rolls

Makes 12 egg rolls
Cook time: 12 minutes

INGREDIENTS

- Cooking oil spray
- 2 garlic cloves, minced
- 340 g minced pork
- 1 teaspoon sesame oil
- 60 ml soy sauce
- 2 teaspoons grated peeled fresh ginger
- 475 ml shredded green cabbage
- 4 spring onions, green parts (white parts optional), chopped
- 24 egg roll wrappers

DIRECTIONS

1. Spray a skillet with the cooking oil and place it over medium-high heat. Add the garlic and

cook for 1 minute until fragrant.

2. Add the minced pork to the skillet. Using a spoon, break the pork into smaller chunks.

3. In a small bowl, whisk the sesame oil, soy sauce, and ginger until combined. Add the sauce to the skillet. Stir to combine and continue cooking for about 5 minutes until the pork is browned and thoroughly cooked.

4. Stir in the cabbage and spring onions. Transfer the pork mixture to a large bowl.

5. Lay the egg roll wrappers on a flat surface. Dip a basting brush in water and glaze each egg roll wrapper along the edges with the wet brush. This will soften the dough and make it easier to roll.

6. Stack 2 egg roll wrappers (it works best if you double-wrap the egg rolls). Scoop 1 to 2 tablespoons of the pork mixture into the centre of each wrapper stack.

7. Roll one long side of the wrappers up over the filling. Press firmly on the area with the filling, tucking it in lightly to secure it in place. Fold in the left and right sides. Continue rolling to close. Use the basting brush to wet the seam and seal the egg roll. Repeat with the remaining ingredients.

8. Insert the crisper plate into the basket and the basket into the unit. Preheat the unit by selecting AIR FRY, setting the temperature to 204ºC, and setting the time to 3 minutes. Select START/ STOP to begin.

9. Once the unit is preheated, spray the crisper plate with cooking oil. Place the egg rolls into the basket. It is okay to stack them. Spray them with cooking oil.

10. Select AIR FRY, set the temperature to 204ºC, and set the time to 12 minutes. Insert the basket into the unit. Select START/STOP to begin. 1DIRECTIONS

11. After 8 minutes, use tongs to flip the egg rolls. Reinsert the basket to resume cooking.

12. When the cooking is complete, serve the egg rolls hot.

Mushroom Tarts

Makes 15 tarts
Cook time: 38 minutes

INGREDIENTS

- 2 tablespoons extra-virgin olive oil, divided
- 1 small white onion, sliced
- 227 g shiitake mushrooms, sliced
- ¼ teaspoon sea salt
- ¼ teaspoon freshly ground black pepper
- 60 ml dry white wine
- 1 sheet frozen puff pastry, thawed
- 240 ml shredded Gruyère cheese
- Cooking oil spray
- 1 tablespoon thinly sliced fresh chives

DIRECTIONS

1. Insert the crisper plate into the basket and the basket into the unit. Preheat the unit by selecting

BAKE, setting the temperature to 148ºC, and setting the time to 3 minutes. Select START/STOP to begin.

2. In a heatproof bowl that fits into the basket, stir together 1 tablespoon of olive oil, the onion, and the mushrooms.

3. Once the unit is preheated, place the bowl into the basket.

4. Select BAKE, set the temperature to 148ºC, and set the time to 7 minutes. Select START/STOP to begin.

5. After about 2½ minutes, stir the vegetables. Resume cooking. After another 2½ minutes, the vegetables should be browned and tender. Season with the salt and pepper and add the wine. Resume cooking until the liquid evaporates, about 2 minutes.

6. When the cooking is complete, place the bowl on a heatproof surface.

7. Increase the air fryer temperature to 200ºC and set the time to 3 minutes. Select START/STOP to begin.

8. Unfold the puff pastry and cut it into 15 (3-by-3-inch) squares. Using a fork, pierce the dough and brush both sides with the remaining 1 tablespoon of olive oil.

9. Evenly distribute half the cheese among the puff pastry squares, leaving a ½-inch border around the edges. Divide the mushroom-onion mixture among the pastry squares and top with the remaining cheese.

10. Once the unit is preheated, spray the crisper plate with cooking oil. Working in batches, place 5 tarts into the basket; do not stack or overlap. 1DIRECTIONS

11. Select BAKE, set the temperature to 200ºC, and set the time to 8 minutes. Select START/STOP to begin.

12. After 6 minutes, check the tarts; if not yet golden brown, resume cooking for about 2 minutes more.

13. When the cooking is complete, remove the tarts and transfer to a wire rack to cool. Repeat steps 10, 11, and 12 with the remaining tarts.

14. Serve garnished with the chives.

Crispy Mozzarella Sticks

Serves 4
Cook time: 5 minutes

INGREDIENTS

- 120 ml plain flour
- 1 egg, beaten
- 120 ml panko breadcrumbs
- 120 ml grated Parmesan cheese
- 1 teaspoon Italian seasoning
- ½ teaspoon garlic salt
- 6 Mozzarella sticks, halved crosswise
- Olive oil spray

DIRECTIONS

1. Put the flour in a small bowl.
2. Put the beaten egg in another small bowl.
3. In a medium bowl, stir together the panko, Parmesan cheese, Italian seasoning, and garlic salt.
4. Roll a Mozzarella-stick half in the flour, dip it into the egg, and then roll it in the panko mixture to coat. Press the coating lightly to make sure the breadcrumbs stick to the cheese. Repeat with the remaining 11 Mozzarella sticks.
5. Insert the crisper plate into the basket and the basket into the unit. Preheat the unit by selecting AIR FRY, setting the temperature to 204°C, and setting the time to 3 minutes. Select START/STOP to begin.
6. Once the unit is preheated, spray the crisper plate with olive oil and place a parchment paper liner in the basket. Place the Mozzarella sticks into the basket and lightly spray them with olive oil.
7. Select AIR FRY, set the temperature to 204°C, and set the time to 5 minutes. Select START/STOP to begin.
8. When the cooking is complete, the Mozzarella sticks should be golden and crispy. Let the sticks stand for 1 minute before transferring them to a serving plate. Serve warm.

Authentic Scotch Eggs

Serves 6
Cook time: 11 to 13 minutes

INGREDIENTS

- 680 g bulk lean chicken or turkey sausage
- 3 raw eggs, divided
- 355 ml dried breadcrumbs, divided
- 120 ml plain flour
- 6 hardboiled eggs, peeled
- Cooking oil spray

DIRECTIONS

1. In a large bowl, combine the chicken sausage, 1 raw egg, and 120 ml of breadcrumbs and mix well. Divide the mixture into 6 pieces and flatten each into a long oval.
2. In a shallow bowl, beat the remaining 2 raw eggs.
3. Place the flour in a small bowl.
4. Place the remaining 240 ml of breadcrumbs in a second small bowl.
5. Roll each hardboiled egg in the flour and wrap one of the chicken sausage pieces around each egg to encircle it completely.
6. One at a time, roll the encased eggs in the flour, dip in the beaten eggs, and finally dip in the breadcrumbs to coat.
7. Insert the crisper plate into the basket and the basket into the unit. Preheat the unit by selecting

AIR FRY, setting the temperature to 192ºC, and setting the time to 3 minutes. Select START/ STOP to begin.

8. Once the unit is preheated, spray the crisper plate with cooking oil. Place the eggs in a single layer into the basket and spray them with oil.

9. Select AIR FRY, set the temperature to 192ºC, and set the time to 13 minutes. Select START/ STOP to begin.

10. After about 6 minutes, use tongs to turn the eggs and spray them with more oil. Resume cooking for 5 to 7 minutes more, or until the chicken is thoroughly cooked and the Scotch eggs are browned. 1DIRECTIONS

11. When the cooking is complete, serve warm.

Soft white cheese Stuffed Jalapeño Poppers

Serves 10
Cook time: 6 to 8 minutes

INGREDIENTS

- 227 g soft white cheese, at room temperature
- 240 ml panko breadcrumbs, divided
- 2 tablespoons fresh parsley, minced
- 1 teaspoon chilli powder
- 10 jalapeño peppers, halved and seeded
- Cooking oil spray

DIRECTIONS

1. In a small bowl, whisk the soft white cheese, 120 ml of panko, the parsley, and chilli powder until combined. Stuff the cheese mixture into the jalapeño halves.

2. Sprinkle the tops of the stuffed jalapeños with the remaining 120 ml of panko and press it lightly into the filling.

3. Insert the crisper plate into the basket and the basket into the unit. Preheat the unit by selecting AIR FRY, setting the temperature to 192ºC, and setting the time to 3 minutes. Select START/ STOP to begin.

4. Once the unit is preheated, spray the crisper plate with cooking oil. Place the poppers into the basket.

5. Select AIR FRY, set the temperature to 192ºC, and set the time to 8 minutes. Select START/ STOP to begin.

6. After 6 minutes, check the poppers. If they are softened and the cheese is melted, they are done. If not, resume cooking.

7. When the cooking is complete, serve warm.

Chapter 9 Fast and Easy Everyday Favourites

Cheesy Potato Patties

Serves 8
Cook time: 10 minutes

INGREDIENTS

- 900 g white potatoes
- 120 ml finely chopped spring onions
- ½ teaspoon freshly ground black pepper, or more to taste
- 1 tablespoon fine sea salt
- ½ teaspoon hot paprika
- 475 ml shredded Colby or Monterey Jack cheese
- 60 ml rapeseed oil
- 235 ml crushed crackers

DIRECTIONS

Preheat the air fryer to 182ºC. Boil the potatoes until soft. Dry them off and peel them before mashing thoroughly, leaving no lumps. Combine the mashed potatoes with spring onions, pepper, salt, paprika, and cheese. Mould the mixture into balls with your hands and press with your palm to flatten them into patties. In a shallow dish, combine the rapeseed oil and crushed crackers. Coat the patties in the crumb mixture. Bake the patties for about 10 minutes, in multiple batches if necessary. Serve hot.

Simple and Easy Croutons

Serves 4
Cook time: 8 minutes

INGREDIENTS

- 2 slices bread
- 1 tablespoon olive oil
- Hot soup, for serving

DIRECTIONS

Preheat the air fryer to 200ºC. Cut the slices of bread into medium-size chunks. Brush the air fryer basket with the oil. Place the chunks inside and air fry for at least 8 minutes. Serve with hot soup.

Sweet Corn and Carrot Fritters

Serves 4
Cook time: 8 to 11 minutes

INGREDIENTS

- 1 medium-sized carrot, grated
- 1 brown onion, finely chopped
- 110 g canned sweetcorn kernels, drained
- 1 teaspoon sea salt flakes
- 1 tablespoon chopped fresh coriander
- 1 medium-sized egg, whisked
- 2 tablespoons milk
- 235 ml grated Parmesan cheese
- 60 ml flour
- ⅓ teaspoon baking powder
- ⅓ teaspoon sugar
- Cooking spray

DIRECTIONS

Preheat the air fryer to 176°C. Place the grated carrot in a colander and press down to squeeze out any excess moisture. Dry it with a paper towel. Combine the carrots with the remaining ingredients. Mould 1 tablespoon of the mixture into a ball and press it down with your hand or a spoon to flatten it. Repeat until the rest of the mixture is used up. Spritz the balls with cooking spray. Arrange in the air fryer basket, taking care not to overlap any balls. Bake for 8 to 11 minutes, or until they're firm. Serve warm.

Spinach and Carrot Balls

Serves 4
Cook time: 10 minutes

INGREDIENTS

- 2 slices toasted bread
- 1 carrot, peeled and grated
- 1 package fresh spinach, blanched and chopped
- ½ onion, chopped
- 1 egg, beaten
- ½ teaspoon garlic powder
- 1 teaspoon minced garlic
- 1 teaspoon salt
- ½ teaspoon black pepper
- 1 tablespoon Engevita yeast flakes
- 1 tablespoon flour

DIRECTIONS

Preheat the air fryer to 200°C. In a food processor, pulse the toasted bread to form breadcrumbs. Transfer into a shallow dish or bowl. In a bowl, mix together all the other ingredients. Use your hands to shape the mixture into small-sized balls. Roll the balls in the breadcrumbs, ensuring to cover them well. Put in the air fryer basket and air fry for 10 minutes. Serve immediately.

Simple Pea Delight

Serves 2 to 4
Cook time: 15 minutes

INGREDIENTS

- 235 ml flour
- 1 teaspoon baking powder
- 3 eggs
- 235 ml coconut milk
- 235 ml soft white cheese
- 3 tablespoons pea protein
- 120 ml chicken or turkey strips
- Pinch of sea salt
- 235 ml Mozzarella cheese

DIRECTIONS

Preheat the air fryer to 200ºC. In a large bowl, mix all ingredients together using a large wooden spoon. Spoon equal amounts of the mixture into muffin cups and bake for 15 minutes. Serve immediately.

Easy Roasted Asparagus

Serves 4
Cook time: 6 minutes

INGREDIENTS

- 450 g asparagus, trimmed and halved crosswise
- 1 teaspoon extra-virgin olive oil
- Salt and pepper, to taste
- Lemon wedges, for serving

DIRECTIONS

Preheat the air fryer to 204ºC. Toss the asparagus with the oil, ⅛ teaspoon salt, and ⅛ teaspoon pepper in bowl. Transfer to air fryer basket. Place the basket in air fryer and roast for 6 to 8 minutes, or until tender and bright green, tossing halfway through cooking. Season with salt and pepper and serve with lemon wedges.

Baked Chorizo Scotch Eggs

Makes 4 eggs
Cook time: 15 to 20 minutes

INGREDIENTS

- 450 g Mexican chorizo or other seasoned sausage meat
- 4 soft-boiled eggs plus 1 raw egg
- 1 tablespoon water
- 120 ml plain flour
- 235 ml panko breadcrumbs
- Cooking spray

DIRECTIONS

Divide the chorizo into 4 equal portions. Flatten each portion into a disc. Place a soft-boiled egg in the centre of each disc. Wrap the chorizo around the egg, encasing it completely. Place the encased eggs on a plate and chill for at least 30 minutes. Preheat the air fryer to 182°C. Beat the raw egg with 1 tablespoon of water. Place the flour on a small plate and the panko on a second plate. Working with 1 egg at a time, roll the encased egg in the flour, then dip it in the egg mixture. Dredge the egg in the panko and place on a plate. Repeat with the remaining eggs. Spray the eggs with oil and place in the air fryer basket. Bake for 10 minutes. Turn and bake for an additional 5 to 10 minutes, or until browned and crisp on all sides. Serve immediately.

Rosemary and Orange Roasted Chickpeas

Makes 1 L
Cook time: 10 to 12 minutes

INGREDIENTS

- 1 L cooked chickpeas
- 2 tablespoons vegetable oil
- 1 teaspoon rock salt
- 1 teaspoon cumin
- 1 teaspoon paprika
- Zest of 1 orange
- 1 tablespoon chopped fresh rosemary

DIRECTIONS

Preheat the air fryer to 204°C. Make sure the chickpeas are completely dry prior to roasting. In a medium bowl, toss the chickpeas with oil, salt, cumin, and paprika. Working in batches, spread the chickpeas in a single layer in the air fryer basket. Air fry for 10 to 12 minutes until crisp, shaking once halfway through. Return the warm chickpeas to the bowl and toss with the orange zest and rosemary. Allow to cool completely. Serve.

Crunchy Fried Okra

Serves 4
Cook time: 8 to 10 minutes

INGREDIENTS

- 235 ml self-raising yellow cornmeal (alternatively add 1 tablespoon baking powder to cornmeal)
- 1 teaspoon Italian-style seasoning
- 1 teaspoon paprika
- 1 teaspoon salt
- ½ teaspoon freshly ground black pepper
- 2 large eggs, beaten
- 475 ml okra slices
- Cooking spray

DIRECTIONS

Preheat the air fryer to 204ºC. Line the air fryer basket with parchment paper. In a shallow bowl, whisk the cornmeal, Italian-style seasoning, paprika, salt, and pepper until blended. Place the beaten eggs in a second shallow bowl. Add the okra to the beaten egg and stir to coat. Add the egg and okra mixture to the cornmeal mixture and stir until coated. Place the okra on the parchment and spritz it with oil. Air fry for 4 minutes. Shake the basket, spritz the okra with oil, and air fry for 4 to 6 minutes more until lightly browned and crispy. Serve immediately.

Buttery Sweet Potatoes

Serves 4
Cook time: 10 minutes

INGREDIENTS

- 2 tablespoons butter, melted
- 1 tablespoon light brown sugar
- 2 sweet potatoes, peeled and cut into ½-inch cubes
- Cooking spray

DIRECTIONS

Preheat the air fryer to 204ºC. Line the air fryer basket with parchment paper. In a medium bowl, stir together the melted butter and brown sugar until blended. Toss the sweet potatoes in the butter mixture until coated. Place the sweet potatoes on the parchment and spritz with oil. Air fry for 5 minutes. Shake the basket, spritz the sweet potatoes with oil, and air fry for 5 minutes more until they're soft enough to cut with a fork. Serve immediately.

Corn Fritters

Serves 6
Cook time: 8 minutes

INGREDIENTS

- 235 ml self-raising flour
- 1 tablespoon sugar
- 1 teaspoon salt
- 1 large egg, lightly beaten
- 60 ml buttermilk
- 180 ml corn kernels
- 60 ml minced onion
- Cooking spray

DIRECTIONS

Preheat the air fryer to 176°C. Line the air fryer basket with parchment paper. In a medium bowl, whisk the flour, sugar, and salt until blended. Stir in the egg and buttermilk. Add the corn and minced onion. Mix well. Shape the corn fritter batter into 12 balls. Place the fritters on the parchment and spritz with oil. Bake for 4 minutes. Flip the fritters, spritz them with oil, and bake for 4 minutes more until firm and lightly browned. Serve immediately.

Easy Devils on Horseback

Serves 12
Cook time: 7 minutes

INGREDIENTS

- 24 small pitted prunes (128 g)
- 60 ml crumbled blue cheese, divided
- 8 slices centre-cut bacon, cut crosswise into thirds

DIRECTIONS

Preheat the air fryer to 204°C. Halve the prunes lengthwise, but don't cut them all the way through. Place ½ teaspoon of cheese in the centre of each prune. Wrap a piece of bacon around each prune and secure the bacon with a toothpick. Working in batches, arrange a single layer of the prunes in the air fryer basket. Air fry for about 7 minutes, flipping halfway, until the bacon is cooked through and crisp. Let cool slightly and serve warm.

Purple Potato Chips with Rosemary

Serves 6
Cook time: 9 to 14 minutes

INGREDIENTS

- 235 ml Greek yoghurt
- 2 chipotle chillies, minced
- 2 tablespoons adobo or chipotle sauce
- 1 teaspoon paprika
- 1 tablespoon lemon juice
- 10 purple fingerling or miniature potatoes
- 1 teaspoon olive oil
- 2 teaspoons minced fresh rosemary leaves
- ⅛ teaspoon cayenne pepper
- ¼ teaspoon coarse sea salt

DIRECTIONS

Preheat the air fryer to 204°C. In a medium bowl, combine the yoghurt, minced chillies, adobo sauce, paprika, and lemon juice. Mix well and refrigerate. Wash the potatoes and dry them with paper towels. Slice the potatoes lengthwise, as thinly as possible. You can use a mandoline, a vegetable peeler, or a very sharp knife. Combine the potato slices in a medium bowl and drizzle with the olive oil; toss to coat. Air fry the chips, in batches, in the air fryer basket, for 9 to 14 minutes. Use tongs to gently rearrange the chips halfway during cooking time. Sprinkle the chips with the rosemary, cayenne pepper, and sea salt. Serve with the chipotle sauce for dipping.

Herb-Roasted Veggies

Serves 4
Cook time: 14 to 18 minutes

INGREDIENTS

- 1 red pepper, sliced
- 1 (230 g) package sliced mushrooms
- 235 ml green beans, cut into 2-inch pieces
- 80 ml diced red onion
- 3 garlic cloves, sliced
- 1 teaspoon olive oil
- ½ teaspoon dried basil
- ½ teaspoon dried tarragon

DIRECTIONS

Preheat the air fryer to 176°C. In a medium bowl, mix the red pepper, mushrooms, green beans, red onion, and garlic. Drizzle with the olive oil. Toss to coat. Add the herbs and toss again. Place the vegetables in the air fryer basket. Roast for 14 to 18 minutes, or until tender. Serve immediately.

Scalloped Veggie Mix

Serves 4
Cook time: 15 minutes

INGREDIENTS

- 1 Yukon Gold or other small white potato, thinly sliced
- 1 small sweet potato, peeled and thinly sliced
- 1 medium carrot, thinly sliced
- 60 ml minced onion
- 3 garlic cloves, minced
- 180 ml 2 percent milk
- 2 tablespoons cornflour
- ½ teaspoon dried thyme

DIRECTIONS

Preheat the air fryer to 192°C. In a baking pan, layer the potato, sweet potato, carrot, onion, and garlic. In a small bowl, whisk the milk, cornflour, and thyme until blended. Pour the milk mixture evenly over the vegetables in the pan. Bake for 15 minutes. Check the casserole—it should be golden brown on top, and the vegetables should be tender. Serve immediately.

Peppery Brown Rice Fritters

Serves 4
Cook time: 8 to 10 minutes

INGREDIENTS

- 1 (284 g) bag frozen cooked brown rice, thawed
- 1 egg
- 3 tablespoons brown rice flour
- 80 ml finely grated carrots
- 80 ml minced red pepper
- 2 tablespoons minced fresh basil
- 3 tablespoons grated Parmesan cheese
- 2 teaspoons olive oil

DIRECTIONS

Preheat the air fryer to 192°C. In a small bowl, combine the thawed rice, egg, and flour and mix to blend. Stir in the carrots, pepper, basil, and Parmesan cheese. Form the mixture into 8 fritters and drizzle with the olive oil. Put the fritters carefully into the air fryer basket. Air fry for 8 to 10 minutes, or until the fritters are golden brown and cooked through. Serve immediately.

Cheesy Baked Grits

Serves 6
Cook time: 12 minutes

INGREDIENTS

- 180 ml hot water
- 2 (28 g) packages instant grits
- 1 large egg, beaten
- 1 tablespoon butter, melted
- 2 cloves garlic, minced
- ½ to 1 teaspoon red pepper flakes
- 235 ml shredded Cheddar cheese or jalapeño Jack cheese

DIRECTIONS

Preheat the air fryer to 204°C. In a baking pan, combine the water, grits, egg, butter, garlic, and red pepper flakes. Stir until well combined. Stir in the shredded cheese. Place the pan in the air fryer basket and air fry for 12 minutes, or until the grits have cooked through and a knife inserted near the centre comes out clean. Let stand for 5 minutes before serving.

Traditional Queso Fundido

Serves 4
Cook time: 25 minutes

INGREDIENTS

- 110 g fresh Mexican (or Spanish if unavailable) chorizo, casings removed
- 1 medium onion, chopped
- 3 cloves garlic, minced
- 235 ml chopped tomato
- 2 jalapeños, deseeded and diced
- 2 teaspoons ground cumin
- 475 ml shredded Oaxaca or Mozzarella cheese
- 120 ml half-and-half (60 ml whole milk and 60 ml cream combined)
- Celery sticks or tortilla chips, for serving

DIRECTIONS

Preheat the air fryer to 204°C. In a baking pan, combine the chorizo, onion, garlic, tomato, jalapeños, and cumin. Stir to combine. Place the pan in the air fryer basket. Air fry for 15 minutes, or until the sausage is cooked, stirring halfway through the cooking time to break up the sausage. Add the cheese and half-and-half; stir to combine. Air fry for 10 minutes, or until the cheese has melted. Serve with celery sticks or tortilla chips.

Cheesy Chilli Toast

Serves 1
Cook time: 5 minutes

INGREDIENTS

- 2 tablespoons grated Parmesan cheese
- 2 tablespoons grated Mozzarella cheese
- 2 teaspoons salted butter, at room temperature
- 10 to 15 thin slices serrano chilli or jalapeño
- 2 slices sourdough bread
- ½ teaspoon black pepper

DIRECTIONS

Preheat the air fryer to 164ºC. In a small bowl, stir together the Parmesan, Mozzarella, butter, and chillies. Spread half the mixture onto one side of each slice of bread. Sprinkle with the pepper. Place the slices, cheese-side up, in the air fryer basket. Bake for 5 minutes, or until the cheese has melted and started to brown slightly. Serve immediately.

Baked Cheese Sandwich

Serves 2
Cook time: 8 minutes

INGREDIENTS

- 2 tablespoons mayonnaise
- 4 thick slices sourdough bread
- 4 thick slices Brie cheese
- 8 slices hot capicola or prosciutto

DIRECTIONS

Preheat the air fryer to 176ºC. Spread the mayonnaise on one side of each slice of bread. Place 2 slices of bread in the air fryer basket, mayonnaise-side down. Place the slices of Brie and capicola on the bread and cover with the remaining two slices of bread, mayonnaise-side up. Bake for 8 minutes, or until the cheese has melted. Serve immediately.

Baked Halloumi with Greek Salsa

Serves 4
Cook time: 6 minutes

INGREDIENTS
Salsa:

- 1 small shallot, finely diced
- 3 garlic cloves, minced
- 2 tablespoons fresh lemon juice
- 2 tablespoons extra-virgin olive oil
- 1 teaspoon freshly cracked black pepper
- Pinch of rock salt
- 120 ml finely diced English cucumber
- 1 plum tomato, deseeded and finely diced
- 2 teaspoons chopped fresh parsley
- 1 teaspoon snipped fresh dill
- 1 teaspoon snipped fresh oregano

Cheese:

- 227 g Halloumi cheese, sliced into ½-inch-thick pieces
- 1 tablespoon extra-virgin olive oil

DIRECTIONS

Preheat the air fryer to 192°C. For the salsa: Combine the shallot, garlic, lemon juice, olive oil, pepper, and salt in a medium bowl. Add the cucumber, tomato, parsley, dill, and oregano. Toss gently to combine; set aside. For the cheese: Place the cheese slices in a medium bowl. Drizzle with the olive oil. Toss gently to coat. Arrange the cheese in a single layer in the air fryer basket. Bake for 6 minutes. Divide the cheese among four serving plates. Top with the salsa and serve immediately.

Beetroot Salad with Lemon Vinaigrette

Serves 4
Cook time: 12 to 15 minutes

INGREDIENTS

- 6 medium red and golden beetroots, peeled and sliced
- 1 teaspoon olive oil
- ¼ teaspoon rock salt
- 120 ml crumbled feta cheese
- 2 L mixed greens
- Cooking spray
- Vinaigrette:
- 2 teaspoons olive oil
- 2 tablespoons chopped fresh chives
- Juice of 1 lemon

DIRECTIONS

Preheat the air fryer to 182°C. In a large bowl, toss the beetroots, olive oil, and rock salt. Spray the air fryer basket with cooking spray, then place the beetroots in the basket and air fry for 12 to 15 minutes or until tender. While the beetroots cook, make the vinaigrette in a large bowl by whisking together the olive oil, lemon juice, and chives. Remove the beetroots from the air fryer, toss in the vinaigrette, and allow to cool for 5 minutes. Add the feta and serve on top of the mixed greens.

Air Fried Butternut Squash with Chopped Hazelnuts

Makes 700 ml
Cook time: 20 minutes

INGREDIENTS

- 2 tablespoons whole hazelnuts
- 700 ml butternut squash, peeled, deseeded, and cubed
- ¼ teaspoon rock salt
- ¼ teaspoon freshly ground black pepper
- 2 teaspoons olive oil
- Cooking spray

DIRECTIONS

Preheat the air fryer to 152°C. Spritz the air fryer basket with cooking spray. Arrange the hazelnuts in the preheated air fryer. Air fry for 3 minutes or until soft. Chopped the hazelnuts roughly and transfer to a small bowl. Set aside. Set the air fryer temperature to 182°C. Spritz with cooking spray. Put the butternut squash in a large bowl, then sprinkle with salt and pepper and drizzle with olive oil. Toss to coat well. Transfer the squash in the air fryer. Air fry for 20 minutes or until the squash is soft. Shake the basket halfway through the frying time. When the frying is complete, transfer the squash onto a plate and sprinkle with chopped hazelnuts before serving.

Beery and Crunchy Onion Rings

Serves 2 to 4
Cook time: 16 minutes

INGREDIENTS

- 160 ml plain flour
- 1 teaspoon paprika
- ½ teaspoon bicarbonate of soda
- 1 teaspoon salt
- ½ teaspoon freshly ground black pepper
- 1 egg, beaten
- 180 ml beer
- 350 ml breadcrumbs
- 1 tablespoons olive oil
- 1 large Vidalia or sweet onion, peeled and sliced into ½-inch rings
- Cooking spray

DIRECTIONS

Preheat the air fryer to 182°C. Spritz the air fryer basket with cooking spray. Combine the flour, paprika, bicarbonate of soda, salt, and ground black pepper in a bowl. Stir to mix well. Combine the egg and beer in a separate bowl. Stir to mix well. Make a well in the centre of the flour mixture, then pour the egg mixture in the well. Stir to mix everything well. Pour the breadcrumbs and olive oil in a shallow plate. Stir to mix well. Dredge the onion rings gently into the flour and egg mixture, then shake the excess off and put into the plate of breadcrumbs. Flip to coat both sides well. Arrange the onion rings in the preheated air fryer. Air fry in batches for 16 minutes or until golden brown and crunchy. Flip the rings and put the bottom rings to the top halfway through. Serve immediately.

Cheesy Jalapeño Cornbread

Serves 8
Cook time: 20 minutes

INGREDIENTS

- 160 ml cornmeal
- 80 ml plain flour
- ¾ teaspoon baking powder
- 2 tablespoons margarine, melted
- ½ teaspoon rock salt
- 1 tablespoon granulated sugar
- 180 ml whole milk
- 1 large egg, beaten
- 1 jalapeño pepper, thinly sliced
- 80 ml shredded extra mature Cheddar cheese
- Cooking spray

DIRECTIONS

Preheat the air fryer to 152°C. Spritz the air fryer basket with cooking spray. Combine all the ingredients in a large bowl. Stir to mix well. Pour the mixture in a baking pan. Arrange the pan in the preheated air fryer. Bake for 20 minutes or until a toothpick inserted in the centre of the bread comes out clean. When the cooking is complete, remove the baking pan from the air fryer and allow the bread to cool for a few minutes before slicing to serve.

Classic Latkes

Makes 4 latkes
Cook time: 10 minutes

INGREDIENTS

- 1 egg
- 2 tablespoons plain flour
- 2 medium potatoes, peeled and shredded, rinsed and drained

- ¼ teaspoon granulated garlic
- ½ teaspoon salt
- Cooking spray

DIRECTIONS

Preheat the air fryer to 192°C. Spritz the air fryer basket with cooking spray. Whisk together the egg, flour, potatoes, garlic, and salt in a large bowl. Stir to mix well. Divide the mixture into four parts, then flatten them into four circles. Arrange the circles into the preheated air fryer. Spritz the circles with cooking spray, then air fry for 10 minutes or until golden brown and crispy. Flip the latkes halfway through. Serve immediately.

Classic Poutine

Serves 2
Cook time: 25 minutes

INGREDIENTS

- 2 russet or Maris Piper potatoes, scrubbed and cut into ½-inch sticks
- 2 teaspoons vegetable oil
- 2 tablespoons butter
- ¼ onion, minced
- ¼ teaspoon dried thyme
- 1 clove garlic, smashed
- 3 tablespoons plain flour
- 1 teaspoon tomato paste
- 350 ml beef stock
- 2 teaspoons Worcestershire sauce
- Salt and freshly ground black pepper, to taste
- 160 ml chopped string cheese

DIRECTIONS

Bring a pot of water to a boil, then put in the potato sticks and blanch for 4 minutes. Preheat the air fryer to 204°C. Drain the potato sticks and rinse under running cold water, then pat dry with paper towels. Transfer the sticks in a large bowl and drizzle with vegetable oil. Toss to coat well. Place the potato sticks in the preheated air fryer. Air fry for 25 minutes or until the sticks are golden brown. Shake the basket at least three times during the frying. Meanwhile, make the gravy: Heat the butter in a saucepan over medium heat until melted. Add the onion, thyme, and garlic and sauté for 5 minutes or until the onion is translucent. Add the flour and sauté for an additional 2 minutes. Pour in the tomato paste and beef stock and cook for 1 more minute or until lightly thickened. Drizzle the gravy with Worcestershire sauce and sprinkle with salt and ground black pepper. Reduce the heat to low to keep the gravy warm until ready to serve. Transfer the fried potato sticks onto a plate, then sprinkle with salt and ground black pepper. Scatter with string cheese and pour the gravy over. Serve warm.

Easy Air Fried Edamame

Serves 6
Cook time: 7 minutes

INGREDIENTS

- 680 g unshelled edamame
- 2 tablespoons olive oil
- 1 teaspoon sea salt

DIRECTIONS

Preheat the air fryer to 204ºC. Place the edamame in a large bowl, then drizzle with olive oil. Toss to coat well. Transfer the edamame to the preheated air fryer. Cook for 7 minutes or until tender and warmed through. Shake the basket at least three times during the cooking. Transfer the cooked edamame onto a plate and sprinkle with salt. Toss to combine well and set aside for 3 minutes to infuse before serving.

Garlicky Baked Cherry Tomatoes

Serves 2
Cook time: 4 to 6 minutes

INGREDIENTS

- 475 ml cherry tomatoes
- 1 clove garlic, thinly sliced
- 1 teaspoon olive oil
- ⅛ teaspoon rock salt
- 1 tablespoon freshly chopped basil, for topping
- Cooking spray

DIRECTIONS

Preheat the air fryer to 182ºC. Spritz the air fryer baking pan with cooking spray and set aside. In a large bowl, toss together the cherry tomatoes, sliced garlic, olive oil, and rock salt. Spread the mixture in an even layer in the prepared pan. Bake in the preheated air fryer for 4 to 6 minutes, or until the tomatoes become soft and wilted. Transfer to a bowl and rest for 5 minutes. Top with the chopped basil and serve warm.

Garlicky Knots with Parsley

Makes 8 knots
Cook time: 10 minutes

INGREDIENTS

- 1 teaspoon dried parsley
- 60 ml melted butter
- 2 teaspoons garlic powder
- 1 (312 g) tube refrigerated French bread dough, cut into 8 slices

DIRECTIONS

Preheat the air fryer to 176°C. Combine the parsley, butter, and garlic powder in a bowl. Stir to mix well. Place the French bread dough slices on a clean work surface, then roll each slice into a 6-inch-long rope. Tie the ropes into knots and arrange them on a plate. Brush the knots with butter mixture. Transfer the knots into the air fryer. You need to work in batches to avoid overcrowding. Air fry for 5 minutes or until the knots are golden brown. Flip the knots halfway through the cooking time. Serve immediately.

Garlicky Courgette and Butternut Squash

Serves 4
Cook time: 10 minutes

INGREDIENTS

- 2 large courgette, peeled and spiralized
- 2 large yellow butternut squash, peeled and spiralized
- 1 tablespoon olive oil, divided
- ½ teaspoon rock salt
- 1 garlic clove, whole
- 2 tablespoons fresh basil, chopped
- Cooking spray

DIRECTIONS

Preheat the air fryer to 182°C. Spritz the air fryer basket with cooking spray. Combine the courgette and butternut squash with 1 teaspoon olive oil and salt in a large bowl. Toss to coat well. Transfer the courgette and butternut squash in the preheated air fryer and add the garlic. Air fry for 10 minutes or until tender and fragrant. Toss the spiralized courgette and butternut squash halfway through the cooking time. Transfer the cooked courgette and butternut squash onto a plate and set aside. Remove the garlic from the air fryer and allow to cool for a few minutes. Mince the garlic and combine with remaining olive oil in a small bowl. Stir to mix well. Drizzle the spiralized courgette and butternut squash with garlic oil and sprinkle with basil. Toss to serve.

Honey Bartlett Pears with Lemony Ricotta

Serves 4
Cook time: 8 minutes

INGREDIENTS

- 2 large Bartlett or Anjou pears, peeled, cut in half, cored
- 3 tablespoons melted butter
- ½ teaspoon ground ginger
- ¼ teaspoon ground cardamom
- 3 tablespoons brown sugar
- 120 ml whole-milk ricotta cheese
- 1 teaspoon pure lemon extract
- 1 teaspoon pure almond extract
- 1 tablespoon honey, plus additional for drizzling

DIRECTIONS

Preheat the air fryer to 192ºC. Toss the pears with butter, ginger, cardamom, and sugar in a large bowl. Toss to coat well. Arrange the pears in the preheated air fryer, cut side down. Air fry for 5 minutes, then flip the pears and air fry for 3 more minutes or until the pears are soft and browned. In the meantime, combine the remaining ingredients in a separate bowl. Whip for 1 minute with a hand mixer until the mixture is puffed. Divide the mixture into four bowls, then put the pears over the mixture and drizzle with more honey to serve.

Golden Salmon and Carrot Croquettes

Serves 6
Cook time: 10 minutes

INGREDIENTS

- 2 egg whites
- 235 ml almond flour
- 235 ml panko breadcrumbs
- 450 g chopped salmon fillet
- 160 ml grated carrots
- 2 tablespoons minced garlic cloves
- 120 ml chopped onion
- 2 tablespoons chopped chives
- Cooking spray

DIRECTIONS

Preheat the air fryer to 176ºC. Spritz the air fryer basket with cooking spray. Whisk the egg whites in a bowl. Put the flour in a second bowl. Pour the breadcrumbs in a third bowl. Set aside. Combine the salmon, carrots, garlic, onion, and chives in a large bowl. Stir to mix well. Form the mixture into balls with your hands. Dredge the balls into the flour, then egg, and then breadcrumbs to coat well. Arrange the salmon balls in the preheated air fryer and spritz with cooking spray. Air fry for 10 minutes or until crispy and browned. Shake the basket halfway through. Serve immediately.

Lemony and Garlicky Asparagus

Makes 10 spears
Cook time: 10 minutes

INGREDIENTS

- 10 spears asparagus (about 230 g in total), snap the ends off
- 1 tablespoon lemon juice
- 2 teaspoons minced garlic
- ½ teaspoon salt
- ¼ teaspoon ground black pepper
- Cooking spray

DIRECTIONS

Preheat the air fryer to 204ºC. Line a parchment paper in the air fryer basket. Put the asparagus spears in a large bowl. Drizzle with lemon juice and sprinkle with minced garlic, salt, and ground black pepper. Toss to coat well. Transfer the asparagus in the preheated air fryer and spritz with cooking spray. Air fryer for 10 minutes or until wilted and soft. Flip the asparagus halfway through. Serve immediately.

Spicy Air Fried Old Bay Shrimp

Makes 475 ml
Cook time: 10 minutes

INGREDIENTS

- ½ teaspoon Old Bay or all-purpose seasoning
- 1 teaspoon ground cayenne pepper
- ½ teaspoon paprika
- 1 tablespoon olive oil
- ⅛ teaspoon salt
- 230 g shrimps, peeled and deveined
- Juice of half a lemon

DIRECTIONS

Preheat the air fryer to 200ºC. Combine the seasoning, cayenne pepper, paprika, olive oil, and salt in a large bowl, then add the shrimps and toss to coat well. Put the shrimps in the preheated air fryer. Air fry for 10 minutes or until opaque. Flip the shrimps halfway through. Serve the shrimps with lemon juice on top.

Southwest Corn and Pepper Roast

Serves 4
Cook time: 10 minutes

INGREDIENTS

- For the Corn:
- 350 ml thawed frozen corn kernels
- 235 ml mixed diced peppers
- 1 jalapeño, diced
- 235 ml diced brown onion
- ½ teaspoon ancho chilli powder
- 1 tablespoon fresh lemon juice
- 1 teaspoon ground cumin
- ½ teaspoon rock salt
- Cooking spray
- For Serving:
- 60 ml feta cheese
- 60 ml chopped fresh coriander
- 1 tablespoon fresh lemon juice

DIRECTIONS

Preheat the air fryer to 192°C. Spritz the air fryer with cooking spray. Combine the ingredients for the corn in a large bowl. Stir to mix well. Pour the mixture into the air fryer. Air fry for 10 minutes or until the corn and peppers are soft. Shake the basket halfway through the cooking time. Transfer them onto a large plate, then spread with feta cheese and coriander. Drizzle with lemon juice and serve.